VLR P-51 MUSTANG
VS
JAPANESE FIGHTERS

Japan 1945

CARL MOLESWORTH

OSPREY PUBLISHING
Bloomsbury Publishing Plc
Kemp House, Chawley Park, Cumnor Hill, Oxford, OX2 9PH, UK
Bloomsbury Publishing Ireland Limited,
29 Earlsfort Terrace, Dublin 2, D02 AY28, Ireland
1385 Broadway, 5th Floor, New York, NY 10018, USA
E-mail: info@ospreypublishing.com

OSPREY is a trademark of Osprey Publishing Ltd

First published in Great Britain in 2025

A catalogue record for this book is available from the British Library.

ISBN: PB 9781472866400; eBook 9781472866431; ePDF 9781472866417;
XML 9781472866424

25 26 27 28 29   10 9 8 7 6 5 4 3 2 1

Edited by Tony Holmes
Cover artwork and battlescene by Gareth Hector
Three-views, cockpit views, and armament views by Jim Laurier
Map and tactical diagram by www.bounford.com
Index by Alison Worthington
Typeset by PDQ Digital Media Solutions, UK
Printed by Repro India Ltd

Osprey Publishing supports the Woodland Trust, the UK's leading woodland
conservation charity.

To find out more about our authors and books visit
www.ospreypublishing.com. Here you will find extracts, author interviews,
details of forthcoming events, and the option to sign up for our newsletter.

For product safety related questions contact productsafety@bloomsbury.com

Acknowledgments
The veterans of the USAAF's VII Fighter Command and their family members
who contributed material to one of my previous books made this volume
possible. I drew as well from authors, listed in the bibliography, who have
tilled this ground ahead of me, and I truly appreciate their work. Special
thanks to my friend and fellow author Edward M. Young for his help in
directing me to my major sources of Japanese photographs for this book,
namely the Peter Bowers and John Lambert photo collections at The Museum
of Flight in Seattle. Finally, a note of appreciation goes to the late Frank
Olynyk, whose vast research on American aerial victory claims during World
War II has provided a strong factual underpinning for my books over the
years. Likewise, the late Joe Baugher's website, *USACS-USAAS-USAAC-
USAAF-USAF Military Aircraft Serial Numbers 1908 to Present*, remains an
invaluable resource. And a final tip of the cap to the late Tom Ivie, who
contributed to this book and many other volumes I have written over
the years.

P-51D Mustang cover artwork
Maj Robert W. "Todd" Moore, leading ace of VII Fighter Command, scored
the last of his 12 victories on August 10, 1945 while providing escort for 70
B-29s assigned to attack an arsenal complex in Tokyo. The formation of B-29s
from the 13th BW and P-51s of the 15th and 506th FGs was near the target
when a small number of Japanese fighters attempted to attack the bombers.
Their strike was uncoordinated and ineffective at breaking up the B-29
formation, which continued to the target. Meanwhile, pilots of the 47th FS
bounced the enemy aircraft and damaged four of them. At this point, Maj
Moore, commanding officer of the 45th FS, led his Mustangs in a second
attack on the IJAAF interceptors. After supporting a fellow pilot who flamed a
Ki-100, Moore turned his attention to a Ki-44 "Tojo" and promptly shot it
down. He followed this up by damaging a Ki-43 "Oscar" before reforming his
squadron and safely returning to Iwo Jima. Moore's victim was almost
certainly a "Tojo" from 70th Sentai, as it is known that Capt Kanji Honda,
1st Chutai leader and Sentai executive officer, was killed in action on that day.
(Artwork by Gareth Hector)

A6M7 Zero-sen cover artwork
The 15th and 506th FGs of VII Fighter Command sent off 97 P-51s on
August 3, 1945, in a substantial strafing attack on Japanese airfields in the
Tokyo area. 1Lt Ed Mikes of the 458th FS was flying one of 17 Mustangs hit
by ground fire during the course of the mission, and he bailed out of his
disabled P-51D into the waters of Sagami-Wan. The Americans mounted an
extensive rescue effort, which included a modified B-17 "Super Dumbo" that
dropped a lifeboat, two US Navy PB4Y Privateers and the submarine USS
Aspro, which approached the area in the hope of picking up the downed pilot.
The IJNAF scrambled a flight of 302nd Kokutai A6M7 Zero-sen from Atsugi
led by Lt Yutaka Morioka to oppose the rescue. Morioka did not hesitate to
attack when he encountered a flight of Mustangs from the 457th FS that were
covering the rescue effort. He picked out the fighter flown by 2Lt John J.
Coneff and opened fire. The stricken P-51 fell into the bay as the other
Mustangs countered Morioka's Zero-sen with a head-on pass and chased them
away. As they were clearing the area, the IJNAF fighters made a strafing pass
on 1Lt Mikes in his lifeboat but missed their target. Eventually, *Aspro* picked
up Mikes, and he made his way back to Iwo Jima several weeks later. No trace
of 2Lt Coneff was ever found. (Artwork by Gareth Hector)

Previous page
These pilots made the 15th FG's 47th FS the top-scoring squadron of VII
Fighter Command's first mission over Tokyo on April 7, 1945, with seven
confirmed aerial victories and two aircraft damaged. They are, from left to
right, 1Lt Dick Hintermeier, Capt Ed Markham, 1Lt Eurich Bright, Capt Bob
Down and 1Lt Richard Condrick. For the day, VII Fighter Command received
credit for 26 Japanese aircraft destroyed for the loss of two P-51Ds and one
pilot. The 47th FS maintained its scoring lead throughout the campaign,
tallying 40 confirmed victories by V-J Day. (Author's Collection)

CONTENTS

INTRODUCTION

Although US Army Air Forces (USAAF) P-51D Mustang pilots encountered defending Japanese fighters over the Tokyo area for only about four months at the end

of World War II, their combats were as brutal and unforgiving as any fought in the preceding five-and-a-half years of the conflict. The Mustang, already having established its legendary status in combat over Europe in 1944, took the measure of all the different fighter types operated by the Imperial Japanese Army Air Force (IJAAF) and the Imperial Japanese Naval Air Force (IJNAF), whether the Americans' mission was escorting B-29 bombers, performing fighter sweeps, or attacking ground targets.

The Japanese fighter forces had the advantage of defending a relatively small and well-defined target area, but they were doomed by a flawed command system, obsolete tactics, a shortage of combat-capable pilots, and other factors. The core of the problem lay in the fact that the IJAAF and IJNAF shared responsibility for providing air defense of the Home Islands. Interservice rivalries between the army and navy were present in most combatant nations of World War II, but the situation in Japan was more pronounced, resulting in wasteful duplications of assets and effort at a time when the nation could least afford them.

During VII Fighter Command's aerial campaign against Central Honshu in the spring and summer of 1945 (the air battles over Kyushu are beyond the focus of this volume), its Mustang pilots encountered seven different Japanese single-engined fighter types with performance nearly matching – and in some cases exceeding – the capabilities of their own P-51Ds. As in air combat since its earliest days, the skill of the pilots involved was most often the deciding factor. Here, the Americans had the advantage, as Japanese pilots ranged from a few experienced masters of aerial combat to a predominance of undertrained fledglings. Even the "tail-end Charlies" in a Mustang formation had hundreds of hours in their logbooks and were well-schooled in aerial tactics and gunnery techniques.

Another factor favoring the Americans was the reliability of the P-51D's Packard Merlin engine, compared to the failure-prone powerplants of all Japanese fighters bar the engine fitted to the A6M5. Imagine plunging into an aerial battle with your attention split between the desire to come to grips with the enemy and the worry that your engine was about to expire.

But the very-long-range (VLR) capability of the P-51D was what made the entire campaign possible, allowing its pilots to make the 650-mile flight to Central Honshu, engage the enemy and then fly back to their bases on Iwo Jima in the Bonin Islands. After six to seven hours in their cramped cockpits, exhausted VLR pilots often had to be lifted out of their Mustangs by their groundcrew.

CHRONOLOGY

1939

April 1	First flight of Mitsubishi Experimental 12-Shi Carrier fighter.
June	Nakajima begins design work on Ki-44.

1940

January	Kawasaki obtains blueprints for the Daimler-Benz DB 601A engine. Three examples of the engine are also supplied from Germany.
February	IJAAF contracts Kawasaki to develop Ki-60 and Ki-61 fighters fitted with license-built Ha-40 inline engines.
April	British Purchasing Commission (BPC) contracts North American Aviation (NAA) to create an advanced fighter for Royal Air Force (RAF) service.
April	Mitsubishi submits design for land-based J2M interceptor to JINAF.
July	Mitsubishi A6M1 Zero-sen makes operational debut over China.
August	Ki-44 prototype begins flight testing.
September	IJNAF issues specification for new floatplane fighter. Kawanishi begins design of K-20, later designated N1K1.
October 26	First flight of prototype NAA NA-73X.
November 22	US Army Air Corps (USAAC) establishes the 15th Pursuit Group (PG) at Wheeler Field, Territory of Hawaii.

1941

March	Flight tests of Ki-60 prototype begins. Disappointing results turn focus to Ki-61.
April 23	First flight of production NA-73.
August 24	First XP-51 arrives at Wright Field, Ohio, for testing by USAAF.
September	47th Hiko Chutai formed to evaluate Ki-44 in combat over China and Burma.
December	Kawasaki completes prototype Ki-61-I fighter.
December	Kawanishi proposes land-based version of N1K1 and begins development of X-1 as a private venture.
December	Nakajima begins design of replacement for Type 1 (Ki-43) fighter.
December 7	A6M2 Zero-sen takes part in Japanese attack on Pearl Harbor, Hawaii, prompting US to declare war on Japan and its Axis partners. Several P-40s of the 15th PG intercept.

1942

January	IJAAF orders 40 Ki-44-Is.
February	VII Fighter Command formed to provide air defense for the Territory of Hawaii.
April 18	Early-production Ki-61 intercepts a B-25 Mitchell over Tokyo during the Doolittle Raid.
May	Design study approved for new Nakajima fighter, designated Type 4 (Ki-84).
July 27	NA-73 Mustang I makes combat debut with RAF.
August	Ki-61-Ia production begins.
September	IJAAF officially adopts Ki-44 as Army Type 2 fighter.

October	Mitsubishi J2M2 Raiden accepted for production.	August	First A6M5 Model 52 Zero-sen rolls off Mitsubishi production line.
October 13	First flight of Rolls-Royce Merlin-powered NA-73.	October 23	15th FG enters combat in the Gilbert Islands, its first action since the Pearl Harbor attack.
November 30	First flight of US-built Merlin-powered XP-51B.	November 17	First flight of bubble-canopy XP-51D.
December 31	First flight of Kawanishi X-1 land-based fighter.	December	J2M2 enters service with 381st Kokutai (Air Group), and it will be deployed primarily in defense of the Home Islands.

1943

April	First flight of prototype Nakajima Ki-84.	December 1	USAAF P-51B makes its combat debut with the 354th FG in England.
July	IJNAF accepts first X-1 for testing, soon instructing Kawanishi to proceed with design of N1K1-J Shiden.	December 31	First flight of N1K2-J prototype.

P-51Ds of the 531st FS/21st FG sit on the flightline, probably at Tinian, in March 1945 as their pilots await orders to move up to Iwo Jima. On March 30, after arriving at Iwo Jima's Central Field, Mustang 44-43912 *MISS JACKIE* was wrecked by 1Lt Robert H. Moody when he was caught in a crosswind and ground-looped. The fighter was transferred to a local air service group and stripped for parts. (Author's Collection)

1944

January	Production of Ki-61-Ic, with upgraded armament, commences.
February	First examples of N1K1-J delivered to 341st Kokutai for testing.
March	Mitsubishi and Nakajima start production of A6M5 Model 52 Zero-sen.
March	P-51D begins to replace P-51B/C on NAA production lines.
April	Ki-44 production peaks at 85 aircraft completed during the month.
April	First production Ki-84s delivered to IJAAF.
April 21	21st FG activated at Wheeler Field.
June	First production N1K2-J Shiden-Kai rolls off Kawasaki production line.
August	IJAAF's 22nd Sentai (Regiment) deploys to China with Ki-84s.
October 12	Combat debut of N1K1-J over Formosa.
October 21	506th FG formed at Lakeland, Florida, for VLR operations.
November	XXI Bomber Command commences B-29 raids on Japan.
December	P-51Ds delivered to VII Fighter Command in Hawaii for training in VLR operations.

1945

January	Nakajima delivers last Ki-44, with production totaling 1,223 aircraft.
January	First N1K2-Js reach newly formed 343rd Kokutai at Matsuyama.
February	15th and 21st FGs of VII Fighter Command ship out of Hawaii for deployment to western Pacific.
February 19	US Marine Corps invades Iwo Jima to secure island as base for VLR P-51D operations.
March 6	VII Fighter Command reassigned to Twentieth Air Force, and first P-51Ds arrive at Iwo Jima.
March 11	VII Fighter Command P-51Ds fly first air strike from Iwo Jima, targeting nearby island of Chichi Jima.
April 7	First VLR mission by VII Fighter Command, escorting B-29s to Tokyo. IJAAF Ki-44s and Ki-61s and IJNAF A6M5s and N1K1-2s intercept. P-51D pilots claim 26 victories and Japanese pilots make 17 claims, including three B-29s. Actual losses are fewer on both sides.
May 11	506th FG P-51Ds arrive on Iwo Jima to join VII Fighter Command.
May 28	506th FG flies first mission to Honshu, claiming two aerial victories.
June 1	VII Fighter Command loses 24 P-51D pilots in storm while en route to Japan.
July 16	In its last major engagement of the war, VII Fighter Command claims 25 aerial victories for one P-51 pilot lost.
August 14	One P-51 pilot missing over Honshu on the day Japan accepts unconditional surrender.
September 2	Japanese representatives sign the official Instrument of Surrender, ending World War II.

DESIGN AND DEVELOPMENT

The Mustang pilots of VII Fighter Command encountered a wide variety of Japanese single-engined fighters during their missions over Central Honshu in 1945. Excluded from this work are the Nakajima Type 1 Ki-43-III "Oscar," which was obsolete by then and therefore used mostly for training, and the twin-engined Ki-45 "Nick," Ki-46 "Dinah," and J1N1 "Irving" nightfighters.

James H. "Dutch" Kindelberger, president and general manager of NAA, played a key role in convincing the BPC that his company could build a better fighter than the P-40 Warhawk. (Tony Holmes Collection)

P-51D MUSTANG

In late 1939, the BPC presented NAA, an American aircraft manufacturer based in California, with a proposition. The war with Germany was only a few months old, but the British already felt the need to bolster their fighter force to face the formidable Luftwaffe. Happy with the Harvard advanced trainer aircraft that NAA had begun supplying the RAF pre-war, the British now wanted the company to build them P-40 Warhawk fighters under license from the Curtiss-Wright Corporation. Perhaps to their surprise, James H. "Dutch" Kindelberger, president and general manager of NAA, said no.

It was not that Kindelberger did not want to build fighters for the RAF. He just did not want to build P-40s. Kindelberger was convinced that NAA could build a better fighter than the Warhawk for the British at a competitive price and within an acceptable timeline. His counter-proposal was that NAA would design and build its own fighter, using the same Allison V-1710 inline engine as the P-40, incorporating modern elements not found in the Curtiss fighter. Despite the fact that this would be NAA's first attempt to build a fighter, the British accepted the company's proposal on April 10, 1940. Work on the new aircraft, designated the NA-73 by the manufacturer, began in earnest.

Concurrent with this action, NAA arranged to buy data from Curtiss related to the development of its own next-generation fighter, the XP-46. Ultimately the latter aircraft never went into production, but the information gleaned from its wind tunnel, cooling, and performance testing reduced the amount of time NAA designers needed to produce the NA-73.

The XP-46 data mainly applied to the design of the NA-73 fuselage, especially the placement of the radiator beneath the center section of the wing. With the radiator in that location, the flow of heated air exiting it could be restricted by means of an adjustable flap to create additional pressure that increased thrust by the equivalent of adding 200hp to the engine. Also important was the application of second-degree curve technology to the fuselage, which provided optimum streamlining.

The other major design element NAA engineers incorporated into the NA-73 was the wing's laminar flow airfoil. Based on research done by the National Advisory Committee for Aeronautics, the laminar flow wing was expected to produce a pronounced reduction in drag compared to conventional airfoils of the day. Initially, the design by NAA engineers seemed to exhibit poor stall characteristics in the wind tunnel, but further testing in a larger wind tunnel validated the wing shape. The airflow remained attached to about 40 percent of the NA-73's wing chord – much higher than other airfoils – and reduced the effects of compressibility at high speeds if the wings were maintained in smooth condition.

The NA-73X prototype airframe rolled out of the NAA factory on September 9, 1940, just 120 days after the BPC contract had been signed. After a month's wait for its engine to be installed, the new fighter made its maiden flight on October 26.

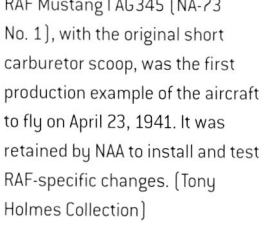

RAF Mustang I AG345 (NA-73 No. 1), with the original short carburetor scoop, was the first production example of the aircraft to fly on April 23, 1941. It was retained by NAA to install and test RAF-specific changes. (Tony Holmes Collection)

F-6Cs, P-51B-1s, and Mustang IIIs sit side-by-side within Hangar No. 2 at Mines Field, California, in early 1944. In the background is P-51B-1 43-12304, which was the second Mustang modified by NAA to incorporate the prototype 85-gallon self-sealing fuselage tank and added oxygen supply. In the foreground is P-51B-1 43-12388, which was the first of three Mustangs to install the production Firestone 85-gallon fuselage tank. (Tony Holmes Collection)

Testing soon made it clear that the aircraft was superior in most respects to the P-40, just as Kindelberger had promised. The British promptly named their new fighter "Mustang" and ordered additional examples. The first production Mustang I flew on April 23, 1941, and the USAAC acquired two from the first batch for testing, designating them XP-51s. Soon, the USAAC followed Britain's lead in ordering Allison-powered Mustangs as A-36A dive-bombers and P-51A fighters.

From the outset, it was clear that the limiting factor in the Mustang's performance was its Allison engine, which lacked sufficient supercharging to produce power at high altitude. To rectify this problem in an otherwise outstanding aircraft, in 1942 NAA engineers began investigating the possibility of mating the Mustang airframe with Britain's legendary Rolls-Royce Merlin engine. With its two-stage mechanical supercharger, the Merlin could produce power at much higher altitudes than the V-1710.

Rolls-Royce was already working at capacity to provide Merlins for the RAF, so the Packard Motor Car Company, an American manufacturer of high-end automobiles, gained permission to produce the engine under license. The Packard V-1650-7 Merlin debuted in the P-51B, along with the addition of an 85-gallon self-sealing fuel tank behind the pilot's seat and the repositioning of the radiator inlet 2.63 inches below the bottom of the wing to improve airflow through the radiator. A four-bladed propeller completed the conversion. With these changes, the Merlin-engined Mustang quickly took its place as the premier high-altitude, long-range fighter of World War II.

By the time VII Fighter Command arrived on Iwo Jima in March 1945, its pilots were flying the P-51D-20 Mustang, the most advanced version of this fighter in service at that time. The three distinguishing features of the D-model Mustang were the bubble canopy for improved vision from the cockpit and easier egress if the pilot needed to bail out, the armament of six wing-mounted 0.50-cal. Browning AN/M2 machine guns and the K-14 or K-14A gyro-computing gunsight.

11

P-51D-25 MUSTANG

32ft 3in.

12ft 2i

37ft 0in.

472 640

501

IJNAF FIGHTERS

The IJNAF used a complex system for designating its aircraft during World War II. The Short Designation tagged each new design with a group of Roman letters and numbers. The first letter indicated the type of aircraft ("A" for carrier fighter and "J" for land-based fighter) followed by a series number for the manufacturer, a letter indicating the manufacturer, and a number for the version of the design. Thus, the A6M5, for example, was the fifth version of Mitsubishi's sixth carrier-based fighter design.

In addition, the IJNAF used a type-and-model system. Each type of aircraft entering production after 1920 was given a type number (the last two digits of the year in the Japanese calendar year) combined with a brief description of its primary function. Only a single digit was used when the year ended in 00, as with the Type 0 Carrier Fighter (thus the name "Zero") which entered production in 1940 or the Japanese year 2600.

Subtypes and new versions of a type were indicated by model numbers added after the type. The Type 0 Carrier Fighter Model 52 was the Zero-sen after five major airframe and two engine configurations. Further modifications to model numbers were indicated by the lower-case Roman letters "a", "b", "c", etc. (i.e. Navy Type 0 Carrier Fighter Model 52c).

In 1943, the IJNAF gave official names to its aircraft in place of type numbers. These names were chosen based on the aircraft's primary role, with carrier fighters (except the Zero-sen) called wind names ending in "pu" or "fu" and land-based fighters getting names for lightning ending in "den."

To avoid confusion in the field, the Allies adopted a simpler system for identifying Japanese aircraft types, with no distinction made between IJNAF and IJAAF types. Fighters received male names, bombers were females, and so on. Although the A6M was the "Zeke" or the "Hamp" in the Allied reporting name system, most pilots who encountered the Mitsubishi fighter called it a "Zero."

VII Fighter Command exclusively flew P-51D-20/25 Mustangs during its brief spell on operations from Iwo Jima, these aircraft being the ultimate model of the NAA fighter to see action with the USAAF in World War II. Here, 44-63909 and 44-72572 (both P-51D-20s) from the 458th FS/ 506th FG await their next mission at North Field. (NARA)

OPPOSITE
P-51D-25 Mustang 44-72640, assigned to Capt Evelyn Neff, features the green striped tail markings of the 506th FG's 457th FS. The pin-up (a topless woman with a flower in her hair) beneath the windscreen was typical of the artwork applied to many of the Mustangs in the 457th FS during the final months of the Pacific War. The fighter also featured the name *MARGIE* on the base of the canopy and an incomplete squadron insignia to the left of the artwork. Neff undertook missions throughout the 506th FG's assignment to VII Fighter Command on Iwo Jima.

13

A6M5 REISEN ("ZEKE")

When the IJNAF gave the A6M1 Reisen (Zero-sen) its combat debut over China in 1940, it should have sent shock waves through the international aviation community. The new aircraft was faster, better armed, more maneuverable, and had a longer range than any other carrier-capable fighter in the world. But it was inconceivable, in the eyes of xenophobic western military leaders and the press, that a supposedly backward nation such as Japan could produce such a fighter. It took the attack on Pearl Harbor on December 7, 1941, and Japan's subsequent advances through Southeast Asia and the South Pacific, to awaken the western world to the capabilities of the Zero-sen.

Westerners should not have been surprised by the aircraft. If they had been paying attention in the late 1930s, they would have known that the A6M's predecessor, the Mitsubishi A5M Type 96 carrier fighter, was also a world-class performer for its day. However, by the time VII Fighter Command Mustangs began ranging over Tokyo in early 1945, the Zero-sen was well beyond its prime and thoroughly outclassed by the sleek American fighter.

Development of the A6M began in October 1937, when the IJNAF released specifications for a new single-seat, carrier-based fighter to replace the A5M. The requirements included a maximum speed of at least 311mph at 13,125ft; climb to 9,840ft in three-and-a-half minutes; endurance of six to eight hours at cruising speed with external drop tank; armament of two 20mm cannon and two 7.7mm machine guns; retractable landing gear; and a two-way radio with direction-finding capability.

Both Nakajima and Mitsubishi expressed interest initially, but when the former dropped out in 1938, the latter was left with a clear field. Jiro Horikoshi, chief designer for Mitsubishi, and his team found that the IJNAF's power loading specification of 5.5lb per one horsepower limited their engine choices to the 875hp Mitsubishi Zuisei 13 and the Nakajima NK1C Sakae 12 with 950hp. The IJNAF chose the Nakajima powerplant, and thus the first production model became the A6M1 Model 11.

Flight testing took place from May through July 1940, and it revealed that Mitsubishi had produced just what the IJNAF and its fighter pilots wanted – a carrier fighter with speed, outstanding maneuverability, and long range. The IJNAF called its new fighter the Reisen, short for "Rei Sentoki," which translates in English as "Zero fighter."

As with any design, however, there were tradeoffs and compromises in the Zero-sen. To achieve its light weight, Horikoshi and his team had sacrificed a robust structure, armor plating, and self-sealing fuel tanks. The first major modification to the fighter was strengthening of the wing spar. In subsequent versions of the Zero-sen, Horikoshi would attempt to improve on each of its weaknesses while maintaining the aircraft's key attributes.

Press reports in 1941 about the performance of new US and British fighter types revealed the need for greater speed in the Zero-sen, so the more powerful Sakae 21 engine was fitted to the new A6M3 Models 22 and 32, along with other modifications. The new models reached IJNAF units in the South Pacific in the summer of 1942, in time to take part in the crucial struggle for the Solomon Islands. Although they were an improvement over the A6M2, the Zero-sen's brief period of dominance over its Allied opponents had run its course.

As the Pacific War progressed into its second year, new American fighters such as the P-38 Lightning, F4U Corsair, and F6F Hellcat changed the nature of air combat against the A6M. Now American pilots were able to exploit the Zero-sen's relatively poor maneuverability and roll rate at high speeds with tactics that avoided low-speed turning combat – the Japanese fighter's forte. To counter this, the IJNAF ordered a new upgrade of the Zero-sen, and Mitsubishi's design team set to work on the project. The result was the A6M5 Model 52.

The IJNAF and its pilots wanted Mitsubishi to build a Zero-sen with better speed and dive characteristics than the existing A6M3. Thus, the major feature of the A6M5 was a new wing with thicker gauge skin and rounded wingtips. The 1,100hp Sakae 21 engine carried over from the A6M3 was fitted with ejector-style exhaust pipes that produced more thrust. Armament also remained the same, with two Type 2 Model 99-2 20mm cannon in the wings and two Type 97 7.7mm machine guns in the nose, synchronized to fire through the propeller.

Service trials began in August 1943, with the new Zero-sen achieving a top speed of 351mph at 19,685ft and a maximum diving speed of 410mph. These were significant improvements, and production of the A6M5 Model 52 began shortly afterwards. Models 52a, 52b, and 52c followed over the next year, each delivering further upgrades. Mitsubishi also developed three follow-up Zero-sen, the A6M7 Model 63, A6M8 Model 54, and A6M8 Model 64. However, only the A6M7 fighter-bomber attained production, and it did not go into service until the last three months of the war.

A captured A6M5 Model 52 in flight, showing the individual exhaust stacks that were a key identifying feature. This example, formerly assigned to 261st Kokutai, was found abandoned at Aslito Field on Saipan in June 1944 and returned to the USA for extensive testing against American fighters. (Tony Holmes Collection)

J2M3 Raiden ("Jack")

Considering that the initial discussions about a new interceptor fighter between Mitsubishi and the IJNAF began in October 1938, the Japanese should have had plenty of time to develop the J2M Raiden ("Thunderbolt") as a fully sorted combat aircraft, available in large numbers, before B-29s began targeting the mainland from the fall of 1944. That did not happen for several reasons.

The IJNAF's 14-Shi specification was a major departure from the previous fighter concept, which produced the lightweight, highly maneuverable A6M Zero-sen. Now the IJNAF wanted a fast, heavily armed point-defense interceptor to protect its land bases from enemy bombing attacks. Mitsubishi, fully involved in refining its A6M design at the time, delayed for nearly a year before getting down to serious work on the J2M.

To achieve the performance required in the specification, the company designed the J2M around its powerful MK4C Kasei 13 radial engine, which produced 1,430hp at takeoff. To offset the weight and large frontal area of the 14-cylinder, twin-row powerplant, Mitsubishi designed a streamlined cowling extending well forward to the propeller, which was connected to the engine by a long shaft. The small opening at the front of the cowling housed a fan that directed cooling air into the engine.

The position of the engine weight toward the middle of the aircraft also allowed for a short rear fuselage, which contributed to the Raiden's stubby appearance. The wing had a low aspect ratio and a laminar flow airfoil section. The latter feature is interesting, considering that NAA has received much more attention for the employment of the laminar flow design in its XP-51 than Mitsubishi has for the J2M during the same time period. Another design feature was the inclusion of Fowler flaps, which could be extended during combat to increase maneuverability.

The prototype J2M1 first flew in March 1942, and testing quickly revealed problems with the new fighter. Although the aircraft remained stable and controllable in flight, the prototype's rate of climb and top speed did not satisfy the IJNAF's 14-Shi requirements. Additionally, the small, curved canopy restricted the pilot's view from the cockpit, the landing gear would not retract at speeds above 100mph, and the mechanism for changing the propeller's pitch frequently failed.

By this time, Japan was at war with the Allies, and Mitsubishi showed considerably more urgency when it rolled out the improved J2M2 Raiden prototype in the summer of 1942. Now the Raiden had a larger windscreen and deeper canopy, a four-bladed propeller and a more powerful engine in the form of the MK4R-A Kasei 23a, which produced 1,870hp at takeoff. The new powerplant gave the fighter the desired performance improvements, but they came at the cost of strong engine vibrations. The IJNAF nevertheless ordered the J2M2 into production while Mitsubishi engineers tackled the vibration problem and other teething issues. Engine vibration improved with the strengthening of the propeller blades and the installation of improved engine mount shock absorbers, but it was never fully resolved.

Production of the J2M2 was slow, and it was not until December 1943 that the IJNAF accepted the first batch of the new fighter for service. As teething problems persisted, only 155 J2M2s were built.

Meanwhile, Mitsubishi was working on an improved Raiden, the J2M3. This version featured an enlarged oil cooler with an internal intake, which was expected to improve engine performance, and upgraded armament consisting of two long-barrel Type 2 Model 99 and two short-barrel Model 1 Type 99 20mm cannon, all mounted in the wings. The fuselage-mounted machine guns seen in earlier Raidens were eliminated. Testing of the J2M3 revealed improved reliability, but the heavier guns sapped speed and rate of climb. Production of the J2M3 commenced in February 1944 while the last of the J2M2s were still being built.

Despite modest improvements with the J2M3, the IJNAF was still disappointed with the Raiden and ordered Mitsubishi to slow its production while concentrating on getting another new fighter, the more promising A7M Reppu ("Hurricane"), ready for service. By the end of the war, around 500 Raidens in all versions had been built. The Reppu never reached production.

N1K2 Shiden-Kai ("George")

The N1K2-J Shiden-Kai ("Violet Lightning") was unique among World War II fighter designs for being the only land-based interceptor developed from a floatplane. The N1K1 Kyofu ("Mighty Wind") was a product of the IJNAF's 15-Shi specification of 1940 for a floatplane fighter that could support operations in the Pacific islands, where land bases were few and far between, replacing the Nakajima-built A6M2-N "Rufe" floatplane. It was only natural that the Kyofu was a Kawanishi design, as that manufacturer's forte was building long-range flying boats.

Service trials of the Kyofu began when the first examples were delivered in August 1942. By then, the nature of the war had changed as the Allies were beginning to contain Japanese forces advancing in the Pacific, diminishing the need for the new fighter. Only 97 were built before Kawanishi halted production in March 1944 to concentrate on developing its land-based version of the Kyofu, the N1K1-J Shiden.

The conversion involved replacing the floats with a retractable landing gear and upgrading the engine from the 1,530hp Mitsubishi MK4E Kasei 15 to Nakajima's 1,820hp NK9B Homare 11 turning a four-bladed propeller. The Shiden showed great promise on paper, but its first flight on 31 December, 1942, was a disappointment. Instead of an expected top speed of 403mph, the fighter could only achieve 357mph, although its other flying characteristics were promising. Its rate of turn was especially good thanks to the aircraft's Kawanishi-designed combat flaps. Perhaps the Shiden's biggest drawback, however, was the main landing gear, which required exceptionally long and complex legs due to the fighter's mid-wing design.

Despite its shortcomings, the N1K1-J earned a production contract from the IJNAF, which viewed the design as a stopgap while Kawanishi worked on an improved version. The first of 1,007 Shidens reached frontline units in early 1944, and most were wiped out – along with the Kyofus – in the ill-fated defense of the Philippines.

To address the problems of the N1K1-J, Kawanishi engineers moved the wing mounting to the bottom of the fuselage, thus allowing the fitment of a shorter and simpler landing gear leg, while lengthening the fuselage and redesigning the tail surfaces. They also simplified construction of the Shiden-Kai by significantly reducing the number of parts – excluding nuts, bolts, and rivets – from 66,000 to 43,000.

Now packing four long-barrel Type 2 Model 99 20mm cannon in the wings, with the fuselage-mounted machine guns deleted, the new fighter was designated the N1K2-J Shiden-Kai. Its 1,990hp NK9H Homare 21 engine and propeller continued

to deliver disappointing outright speed performance, but flying characteristics were excellent. The only caution in that department was that the pilot needed to maintain a gentle touch on the controls as the Shiden-Kai approached its stalling speed. Despite being limited to low-octane fuel, the fighter was still able to operate effectively at altitudes up to 30,000ft. IJNAF evaluators favored the N1K2-J over the Raiden, citing superior range and maneuverability, plus better visibility from the cockpit.

The prototype N1K2-J completed its first flight from the newly constructed Naruo airfield on December 31, 1943, with Kawanishi test pilot Munekichi Okayasu at the controls. Painted orange/yellow overall as per IJNAF regulations, the prototype was photographed on the Naruo flightline wearing the production number "91" in white on its tail. Production aircraft differed very little from this machine, with only the cowling and exhaust stubs being altered. The first 100 N1K2-Js also had the larger tail as seen here, with all subsequent examples having a vertical stabilizer that was 13 percent smaller in area. (Tony Holmes Collection)

Although the IJNAF had planned for a force of 2,000 Shiden-Kai, production was disrupted by the B-29 offensive against Japan. This meant that fewer than 400 N1K2-Js were built. Deliveries of the N1K2-J began in early 1945, and by most accounts it was the best fighter available to the IJNAF in the final months of the war.

IJAAF FIGHTERS

The IJAAF naming system was simpler than the IJNAF's, although it also had multiple components. Both a type number system and a Kitai number system were used, and most fighter types were given an Allied reporting name. After 1939, type numbers were the last digit of the Japanese year in which the type was accepted into service.

The Kitai or Ki ("kee") system assigned a number to each aircraft planned or projected to be built. At first the numbers were assigned sequentially, but in 1944 newly issued Ki numbers were scrambled. New versions of an existing design had Roman numerals (I, II, III, etc.) added to the Ki number, while subvariants had lower-case Roman letters as used in some navy systems. And sometimes, the model and variant numbers and letters were supplanted by a Kaizo (Kai) or modification code. There was no clear pattern for the choice of Allied reporting names for IJAAF fighters.

Ki-44 Shoki ("Tojo")

The oldest aircraft manufacturer in Japan, the Nakajima Aircraft Company had a long history of producing fighters, from biplanes of the 1920s through to the revolutionary all-metal monoplane Ki-27 of 1937 and the Ki-43 Hayabusa ("Peregrine Falcon") of the following year. All these designs favored maneuverability and rate of climb above all other measures of performance. The company's fighters were lightweight, lightly armed, and lacked armor protection for vital areas such as the cockpit, fuel tanks, and engine. The Ki-27's victories against Chinese and Soviet fighters over mainland China in the late 1930s seemed to vindicate its design philosophy.

Times were changing, however. IJAAF planners were aware of the high-speed, heavily armed, multi-engined bombers being developed in the West. Japan would need a heavily armed interceptor with high top speed and a fast rate of climb to higher altitudes if the nation ever faced attack by modern bombers. In 1938, the IJAAF asked Nakajima to produce a new, heavy fighter, which became the Type 2 Ki-44 Shoki ("Devil Queller"). The aircraft would be developed in parallel with the Ki-43, but priority was given to the Hayabusa since there was no imminent threat of attack at that time from nations half-a-world away.

The IJAAF requirement was for a single-seat monoplane fighter that could achieve 373mph at 13,120ft and climb to that altitude in under five minutes. Armament was to be two Type 1 (Ho-103) 12.7mm machine guns and two Type 89 7.7mm machine guns. Nakajima chose to power its new interceptor with its own Ha-41 engine, a two-row, 14-cylinder radial producing 1,250hp. Behind the powerplant was a small airframe with a tapered fuselage and stubby wings – the latter featured butterfly flaps that enhanced high-speed maneuverability.

The first prototype began testing in the summer of 1940, and immediately several problems emerged. It reached a top speed of just 342mph, the rate of climb was slower than specified and the aircraft's landing speed was high. Some of these issues arose from the fact that the Ki-44 tipped the scales at 5,622lb, nearly 800lb above its design weight. Nakajima tried many modifications to improve the Ki-44, including some six changes to the supercharger intake. Eventually, the modified prototype was able to reach 389mph (without armament fitted). The IJAAF instructed Nakajima to build seven pre-production aircraft to be completed by the summer of 1941 and delivered to newly formed 47th Chutai (independent air company) for service trials.

47th Chutai took its new Shokis to Canton, China, and then moved to French Indochina at the end of the year to support the Japanese invasion of Malaya. As might be expected, the Ki-44s exhibited serviceability problems, but 47th Chutai also scored the new fighter's first aerial victory. The evaluation was completed in September 1942 following flight testing against the new Ki-43-IIa and Ki-61, an imported Bf 109E and a captured P-40E. The Ki-44 exhibited an excellent rate of roll and a notable turn of speed in a dive, and the evaluators rated it second behind the Ki-61.

Despite the Shoki's good showing in competitive flight testing, the IJAAF felt it would need major upgrades before the aircraft could be considered ready for frontline service. Prototypes of an updated version, the Ki-44-II, would feature the more powerful Ha-109 engine (1,520hp at takeoff), armor protection for vital areas of the airframe and a stronger undercarriage. Production started in November 1942.

The IJAAF ordered 40 Ki-44-Is in January 1942, and the aircraft was officially adopted as the Army Type 2 fighter that September. Production peaked at 85 aircraft completed during April 1944. These Shokis were assigned to 70th Sentai. (Peter M. Bowers Collection/Museum of Flight)

The Ki-44-II Otsu followed, with its weaponry increased to four 12.7 mm machine guns, and this became the principal version of the Shoki. Armament received another upgrade in the Ki-44-II Hei, which carried two Ho-301 40mm or Ho-203 37mm wing cannon plus two 12.7mm machine guns in the fuselage. The Hei's effectiveness was hindered by its ability to carry only 25 rounds for each of the wing cannons, and few were built. The Ki-44-II remained in production until December 1944, by which time 1,225 had been delivered. Shokis served through to the end of the war.

Ki-61 Hein ("Tony")

Kawasaki's handsome Ki-61 Hein ("Swallow") was developed not so much in response to IJAAF performance requirements, but because of the availability and potential of its engine. In the end, that engine led to its demise. The company's history of building V12-powered aircraft dated back to 1923, when it obtained a license to build a BMW liquid-cooled engine of this size that would power bombers, fighters, and reconnaissance aircraft throughout the next decade. After 1933, Kawasaki built a total of 1,400 Ki-10 biplane fighters and Ki-32 light bombers, also powered by the company's license-built Ha-9 V12 engine. This was a remarkable accomplishment, considering the IJAAF's oft-stated preference for radial engines.

Kawasaki stayed the course as the 1930s progressed, and in March 1938 the company obtained manufacturing rights for the new Daimler-Benz inverted V12 inline liquid-cooled engine. A team of Kawasaki engineers traveled to Germany in April 1940 in preparation for license-production of the company's own version of the DB 601A, returning to Japan with a full set of blueprints and several assembled engines. Soon they produced the Ha-40, which generated slightly more power and was a little lighter than the Daimler-Benz engine.

The IJAAF designated the Ha-40 as its Army Type 2 engine and instructed Kawasaki to produce two fighters designed around the powerplant – a heavy interceptor, which became the Ki-60, and the Ki-61 all-purpose fighter. The former was developed first, although it was soon dropped due to excessive wing loading that restricted its maneuverability beyond the level the IJAAF would accept.

Following the abandonment of the Ki-60, the emphasis switched to the Ki-61 in December 1940. Kawasaki chief engineer Takeo Doi and his team were responsible for this aircraft, and their primary goal was to improve its maneuverability over the Ki-60. To do this, they designed a high-aspect wing with increased area for more lift, reduced weight with a smaller cross-section fuselage, and streamlined the nose. The radiator, as with NAA's P-51, sat beneath the fuselage near the center of gravity. Armament was two Type 1 (Ho-103) 12.7mm machine guns in the nose and two Type 89 7.7mm machine guns in the wings.

When the first prototype was finally rolled out in December 1941, it was actually larger and heavier than the Ki-60. Initial flight testing revealed that the Ki-61 was a much better aircraft, however, being both faster and more maneuverable than its predecessor, with excellent controllability in a high-speed dive. A pre-production Ki-61 won the competitive fly-off previously mentioned in the Ki-44 section, reaching a top speed of 367mph at 19,685ft. The IJAAF issued a production contract for an initial batch of the aircraft, designated the Ki-61-Ia Hein Type 3 Army Fighter.

From the beginning, the fighter's weak point was its unreliable Ha-40 engine, which suffered from faulty fuel and oil systems and failure of the main bearings. Production of Ki-61s proceeded at a crawl as Kawasaki struggled to remedy these issues – only 34 had been completed by the end of 1942. Engine unreliability would continue to plague the Hein throughout its service life, although the IJAAF saw enough potential in the design to order a series of upgraded versions.

The first of these was the Ki-61-Ib, with an increased armament of four 12.7mm machine guns. Seeking more firepower, the IJAAF next ordered the Ki-61-I KAI, which replaced the machine guns in the wings with two Ho-5 20mm cannon. Further changes in the KAI variant were a longer fuselage, fixed tailwheel, stronger wings, and the addition of underwing pylons for mounting expendable fuel tanks or bombs. This became the most numerous version of the Hein. Production of the Ki-61-I was phased out in December 1944 after 2,734 had been built.

In general, IJAAF fighter pilots were content with the Ki-61, appreciating its performance, firepower, and armor protection, while they had no choice but to accept its unreliable engine. When all systems were functioning properly, a well-flown Hein was a match for any Allied fighter it was likely to meet in combat.

Seeking to fulfill the IJAAF's request for a Hein with higher performance, Kawasaki engineers produced the new Ha-140 version of their V12 engine, which generated 1,500hp at takeoff, and redesigned the airframe to handle the additional power. The first Ki-61-II prototype, delivered in August 1943, featured a wing with increased span and a new canopy for improved vision. Frustratingly, the new engine proved just as unreliable as the old one, and flight testing was disappointing due to wing failures and poor handling characteristics. Kawasaki reverted to the Ki-61-I wing, lengthened the fuselage again and increased the rudder area to create the Ki-61-II KAI. Flight testing began in April 1944, and the new fighter flew well when the engine was running properly. A little over 400 were built.

Ki-84 Hayate ("Frank")

When the IJAAF delivered Nakajima's outstanding Ki-84 Hayate ("Gale") to its pilots in 1944, they finally had a fighter that could go head-to-head with any Allied interceptor they met in combat. The aircraft could trace its roots back to Nakajima's designs for the Type 3 fighter of 1941. Although the company had lost that competition

This Ki-61-I was probably one of the earliest production models on a test flight – perhaps serial number 114, manufactured in September 1942. The spinner is unpainted and there appears to be no anti-glare panel. The Hein was the only Japanese fighter powered by an inline, liquid-cooled engine, its Kawasaki Ha-40 being a license-built version of Germany's Daimler-Benz DB 601A. The Ki-61 was heavily armed and performed well, but it suffered from chronic engine reliability problems. (Tony Holmes Collection)

The Ki-84 combined the armament of a "heavy fighter" with the excellent maneuverability of a "light fighter", with superior performance from the 1,800hp Nakajima Ha-45 Homare engine. This early Service trials Ki-84 was photographed serving with the Tachikawa Army Air Arsenal in 1943. (Peter M. Bowers Collection/ Museum of Flight)

to Kawasaki's Ki-60 and Ki-61, its engineers had learned a lot about state-of-the-art fighter design and were therefore ready in January 1942 when the IJAAF issued specifications for the Type 4 long-range, all-purpose aircraft to replace the Ki-43 in the fighter-versus-fighter role. Their product, the Ki-84, turned out to be one of the best propeller-driven fighters developed by any country during World War II.

Nakajima's design team set itself the goal of producing a fighter that would be more maneuverable than the Ki-44 and boast a top speed of 400–425mph. Its powerplant would be Nakajima's new, 18-cylinder Ha-45 radial, which was rated at 1,800hp. The Ki-84 featured armor protection for vital areas of the airframe, self-sealing fuel tanks, combat flaps, and armament consisting of two fuselage-mounted Type 1 (Ho-103) 12.7mm machine guns and two wing-mounted Ho-5 20mm cannon.

The designers worked fast, and the new prototype made its first flight in April 1943 at Ojima. When initial tests proved promising, the IJAAF made a change in its acquisition procedures to speed progress toward the service introduction of the Hayate. Whereas previously the IJAAF would order service test aircraft in small numbers and tweak the design before procuring the next batch, for the Ki-84 it ordered 125 pre-production machines. This would allow design modifications to proceed at the same time pilots were undergoing transition training on their new mounts. The first batch of 83 Ki-84s was built between August 1943 and March 1944.

When the prototype's speed topped out at 388mph, designers added individual exhaust stacks to the engine. The new pipes augmented thrust and added about 10mph to the top speed. Other changes improved takeoff handling and added wing racks outboard of the landing gear to carry drop tanks or bombs. Production Hayates, designated Ki-84-Ias, began rolling out of the Nakajima factory in April 1944 and made their combat debut with 22nd Sentai over China four months later. By the end of the year, 11 Sentai were flying Hayates in combat, primarily over the Philippines.

Although the Ki-84s exhibited excellent performance against the Allied fighters they opposed, certain problems arose that the Nakajima engineers sought to address. Pilots felt the landing gear struts were weak, and they also reported failures of the fuel and hydraulic systems. But the most vexing problems had to do with the Ha-45 engine, which failed to produce the rated power required with the low-octane fuel available in combat zones and was also prone to mechanical failure due to poor manufacturing processes. An improved version of the engine in the form of the fuel-injected Ha-45-23, with 2,000hp, powered the upgraded Ki-84-Ib, which also featured heavier armament with two Ho-5 20mm cannon in the wings and two more replacing the machine guns in the fuselage. Its top speed reached a respectable 416mph with high-octane fuel.

In all, 3,400 Hayates were built in the final 18 months of the war. This was a remarkable achievement, considering that repeated B-29 attacks on Nakajima's factories forced it to disperse production to satellite plants during 1945.

Ki-84-I HAYATE

32ft 10in.

11ft 1.25in.

36ft 10in.

715

Ki-100 (no Allied reporting name)

As Kawasaki struggled to work out the reliability problems with its new Ha-140 in the fall of 1944, completed Ki-61-II airframes destined to be powered by the engine began stacking up at the company's Gifu and Ichinomiya assembly plants. The IJAAF, desperate for fighters to deploy in defense of the Home Islands, directed Kawasaki in November 1944 to fit Mitsubishi Ha-112-II radial engines to 275 engineless Heins and get them into service.

Converting the slim Hein fuselage to radial power was no small task because the diameter of the big engine, rated at 1,500hp, was four feet, while the cross-section of the Hein was a slim 2.5ft. Drawing inspiration from an imported Focke-Wulf Fw 190A at their disposal, the Kawasaki designers crafted the engine mount, a compact cowling and fairing, along with a redesigned propeller. The first prototype took flight in February 1945 after a remarkably short two months of development.

The new aircraft, designated Ki-100-Ia Type 5 Army Fighter, was an immediate success. Not only was it faster than the Ki-61, it also had a superior rate of climb and increased maneuverability. Furthermore, its radial engine made the aircraft more reliable and easier to maintain in the field. With two Type 1 (Ho-103) 12.7mm machine guns in the fuselage and two Ho-5 20mm cannon in the wings, the Ki-100 was heavily armed as well.

The IJAAF ordered Kawasaki to convert its 275 engineless Ki-61-IIs to Ki-100s, and then commence building Ki-100s from scratch, which began in June. The scratch-built Ki-100-Ib featured a cutdown rear fuselage with improved rear-vision canopy, but only 99 were completed before bombing raids destroyed Kawasaki's manufacturing plants.

The Ki-100 went into frontline service in March 1945, and it quickly became a favorite amongst IJAAF pilots. The aircraft's combat successes were limited by the small number of Ki-100s deployed and the nature of the air war over Japan in the closing months of the conflict, but today it is remembered for rivaling Nakajima's Ki-84 for the title of the finest Japanese fighter of World War II.

Developed in the closing months of the war by combining the Ki-61 airframe with a 1,500hp Mitsubishi Ha-112-II radial engine, the Ki-100 was a surprising success. It outperformed the Ki-61 and was also more reliable. These Ki-100-Ias of 59th Sentai were captured intact at war's end, the fighters being marked with the colors of the unit's 1st Chutai. (Tony Holmes Collection)

TECHNICAL
SPECIFICATIONS

P-51D-20/25 MUSTANG

When the 15th and 21st FGs of VII Fighter Command arrived on Iwo Jima in early March 1945, they were fully equipped with P-51D-20 Mustangs. The 506th FG, with P-51D-20s and D-25s, arrived two months later. These aircraft were the latest versions of the Merlin-powered Mustang, which had made its combat debut over Europe in

A mix of P-51D-20s and D-25s from the 46th FS/21st FG sit in a row on the flightline with three B-24s in the background. *Okey Dokey* and the third Mustang are D-25s, while 44-63432 between them is a D-20. A newer aircraft, '211' displays just three VLR mission markers forward of the cockpit. (Author's Collection)

P-51D-20 ARMAMENT

The P-51D-20/25 was armed with six free-firing 0.50-cal. Browning AN/M2 machine guns, three weapons in each wing. They were charged manually on the ground and fired simultaneously when the trigger switch on the control column grip was pressed. The maximum ammunition capacity for each of the inboard guns was 400 rounds, with 270 for the center and outboard guns. The weapons were adjustable on the ground and could be harmonized to different patterns for various tactical situations. They were usually aligned to converge at a range of 250–300 yards.

OPPOSITE

IJNAF technicians swarm over an A6M5 Reisen to prepare the fighter for its next flight. Although this variant was several hundred pounds heavier than the preceding A6M3, its 1,100hp Nakajima NK1F Sakae 21 twin-row radial gave the A6M5 a higher top speed of 351mph at 19,685ft. (Peter M. Bowers Collection/ Museum of Flight)

December 1943. NAA made numerous improvements through the P-51B/C series before debuting the P-51D-5, with its iconic bubble canopy and six-gun armament, in mid-1944. Of the roughly 15,000 Mustangs built, more than half were P-51Ds.

Aside from its innovative radiator mounting under the fuselage and the laminar-flow airfoil of its wing, the P-51D was a conventional single-engined, single-seat, all-metal fighter design. Only the rudder was fabric-covered. A Packard V-1650-7 liquid-cooled V12 engine provided power. A license-built version of the Rolls-Royce Merlin 60 with a two-stage, two-speed supercharger, the engine produced 1,490hp and drove a Hamilton Standard 11.2ft four-bladed propeller. Armament consisted of six 0.50-cal. AN/M2 "light-barrel" M2 Browning machine guns mounted in the wings. The inner pair of guns had 400 rounds per weapon, and the remaining four had 270, for a total of 1,880 rounds. A K-14 "ace maker" gunsight was standardized on the P-51D-20, and the P-51D-25 had five zero-length rocket rails beneath each wing and AN/APG-13 tail warning radar.

It could be said that in the P-51D, the whole was even greater than the sum of its parts. It was fast at 437mph, had a high service ceiling of 41,900ft, and was reasonably maneuverable. But what made the P-51D ideal for its assignment on Iwo Jima was its

LEFT
An armorer of the 72nd FS/ 21st FG inspects the 0.50-cal. ammunition stored in the wing trays of a Mustang on Iwo Jima. P-51D armament consisted of six 0.50-cal. AN/M2 "light-barrel" M2 Browning machine guns mounted in the wings. The inner pair of guns had 400 rounds per weapon, and the remaining four had 270 each. (Author's Collection)

RIGHT
VII Fighter Command's P-51D-25s carried high-velocity aerial rockets on VLR missions for the first time on May 25, 1945. Here, a groundcrewman fills one of the 165-gallon drop tanks attached to Mustang '129' of the 78th FS/ 15th FG. The extra weight and drag imposed by the rockets necessitated the use of oversized drop tanks to give the Mustangs the range they needed to complete the mission. (Author's Collection)

range. With full internal fuel and two 110-gallon drop tanks, the Mustang could fly 760 miles from Iwo Jima to Tokyo, fight at full throttle for about 15 minutes, and then fly home with enough fuel in reserve to allow for minor miscalculations in navigation. With the P-51D, American pilots had a fighter fully capable of out-dueling anything the Japanese could throw at them.

A6M5 REISEN ("ZEKE")

The fact that the Mitsubishi A6M fighter was still in frontline service with the IJNAF in 1945 is proof of the difficulties that Japanese aircraft manufacturers had in developing more modern types during World War II. The capabilities that the A6M2 exhibited over Pearl Harbor and the Philippines in December 1941 – speed, maneuverability, range, and firepower – had stunned the western world. But despite a series of upgrades to the aircraft throughout the war, it was no longer capable of dominating Allied opponents three years later. More advanced US Navy and USAAF fighters combined with improved tactics employed by the pilots who flew them left the A6M behind. Although Mitsubishi designers tried, there simply was not enough "stretch" in the original design to keep pace.

The A6M5 was an all-metal, single-seat monoplane with fabric-covered control surfaces and a semi-monocoque fuselage. Aside from the exhaust stacks, the fuselage of the A6M5 looked much like its predecessor, the A6M3. The major difference was in the wings. Both models had the same wingspan, but the A6M5's wing featured rounded tips, with thicker gauge aluminum skinning and ailerons faired into the wingtips.

Also carried over from the A6M3 was the engine, a Nakajima NK1F Sakae 21 twin-row radial with 1,100hp, and the propeller, a three-bladed Hamilton Standard constant-speed, variable pitch design built under license by Sumitomo. Armament varied, with the A6M5c packing the heaviest punch – three Type 3 13.2mm machine guns, one in the upper fuselage decking firing through the propeller and two in the wings, the latter alongside two Type 99 20mm cannon. Some 7,460 A6M5s were built.

Although the A6M5 was several hundred pounds heavier than its predecessor, the upgraded fighter had a higher top speed of 351mph at 19,685ft and an improved maximum diving speed of 410mph. The added weight hampered maneuverability slightly, but the A6M5's wing loading was still superior to the Mustang's. However, its top speed and maximum velocity in a dive fell far short of the P-51D.

J2M3 RAIDEN ("JACK")

Stubby in appearance and few in number, the Mitsubishi J2M might have been a game-changing interceptor if its reliability woes could have been conquered. But they were not. Its 1,820hp Mitsubishi MK4R-A Kasei 23a radial engine remained prone to failure throughout the war, causing vexation for its pilots and frustration for their commanders.

A6M5 ARMAMENT

The A6M5 Model 52 retained the basic armament of the earlier Zero-sen variants, with two Type 97 7.7mm machine guns in the nose. Ammunition boxes held 700 rounds per gun. The two Type 99-2 20mm cannon in the wings featured longer barrels than the earlier Type 99-1, with approximately 18in. of the weapon extending forward of the wing leading edge. The Model 52's cannon were drum-fed, with a drum containing 100 rounds for each weapon.

As a point-defense interceptor, the J2M was a departure from previous IJNAF fighter designs, favoring a high rate of climb, high-altitude capability, and heavy armament over maneuverability and range. An all-metal, low-wing monoplane with a wide-set main landing gear, its wingspan measured 35ft 2.5in. and the fuselage (J2M3) was 32ft 7in. long. Despite a takeoff weight of 7,573lb, the Raiden could climb to 19,658ft a minute-and-a-half quicker than the A6M and had a higher top speed at 380mph. When it reached combat altitude, the Raiden had enough firepower with four Type 99 20mm cannon to do serious damage to any adversary, even the B-29s it faced over Japan in 1944–45.

With a competent pilot in the cockpit and the Kasei engine running at full song, the J2M3 was a worthy opponent for VII Fighter Command's P-51Ds. Fortunately for the Mustang pilots, meeting a Raiden under these conditions did not happen very often.

N1K2-J Shiden-Kai ("George")

On paper, Kawanishi's N1K2-J Shiden-Kai, with a slower top speed, lower service ceiling, and higher wing loading than the J2M3, appears to be the second-best IJNAF interceptor faced by VII Fighter Command Mustangs over Honshu in 1945. But the differences were so slight as to be barely significant.

N1K2-J ARMAMENT

Like the N1K1-J before it, the N1K2-J featured four Type 2 99 Model 2 Mark 4 20mm cannon. However, unlike the Shiden, which had two weapons mounted in the wings and two in underwing gondolas, all four of the Shiden-Kai's weapons were installed within the fighter's wing structure. The magazines for the inner cannon contained 200 rounds per gun, while the outer magazines had space for 100 rounds per weapon.

As a follow-on design from the earlier mid-wing N1K1-J Shiden, the N1K2-J incorporated several changes that made it a more suitable aircraft for frontline service. The aircraft's repositioned low wing allowed Kawanishi to rework the Shiden's long and troublesome main landing gear into a more dependable unit. Other visible changes included a longer semi-monocoque fuselage and reshaped fin and rudder. The wingspan was 36ft 1in., its fuselage measured 30ft 7in. in length and the takeoff weight was 10,714lb. The fighter's Nakajima NK9H Homare 21 engine produced a healthy 1,990hp and drove a four-bladed propeller, but it was hampered by unavailability of high-octane fuel to produce full power. Hydraulically-operated Fowler flaps were fitted, along with fabric-covered ailerons and rudder. Armament, like the J2M3, was four Type 99 20mm cannon in the wings.

As with all late-war Japanese fighters, the N1K2-J was significantly slower than the P-51D, with a top speed of 369mph at 18,375ft. Its service ceiling of 35,300ft was also less than that achievable in a Mustang, but this rarely factored into combat situations. The Shiden-Kai handled relatively well at lower speeds, with a good roll rate and rate of turn, plus a rate of climb of 2,200ft per minute at 8,000ft. But the ailerons became heavy as the Shiden-Kai approached maximum speed, reducing roll rate and unbalancing the controls, with light rudder and elevator pressures compared to the heavy ailerons. Stall characteristics were considered poor at all speeds.

Ki-44-IIb ARMAMENT

The Ki-44-IIb's armament of two cowling-mounted Type 89 7.7mm machine guns (each with magazines containing 500 rounds per weapon) and two wing-mounted Ho-103 12.7mm machine guns (250 rounds per weapon) was extremely light when compared to the USAAF and US Navy fighters it met in the skies over Japan in 1945. Rate of fire for the 12.7mm was 800 rounds per minute, while the synchronized 7.7mm gun was just 400 rounds per minute.

Ki-44-IIb Shoki ("Tojo")

With its big engine and small airframe, the Ki-44 Shoki was the only IJAAF fighter designed specifically for bomber interception. It had had some success in this role earlier in the war over China and the South Pacific, but when the B-29 Superfortresses began ranging over the Home Islands in 1944, the aircraft lacked sufficient high-altitude performance and firepower to succeed at its mission. The introduction of P-51D escort fighters in April 1945 only made matters worse for Shoki pilots.

The Ki-44-IIb (also known as the Ki-44-II-Hei) was an all-metal design with fabric-covered control surfaces and butterfly flaps that could be extended in combat to reduce the fighter's turning radius. Its stubby wings had a span of 31ft and the fuselage measured 28ft 8.6in. in length. Maximum takeoff weight was 6,598lb. The engine, a Nakajima Ha-109 14-cylinder radial producing 1,520hp, drove a three-bladed metal propeller.

While early models of the Shoki were recognizable by the telescopic gunsight that protruded through the windscreen, the Ki-44-IIb had an improved Army Type 100 reflector gunsight in the cockpit. Armament for a bomber interceptor was light, with two Type 1 (Ho-103) 12.7mm machine guns in the fuselage firing through the

Groundcrew run up a trio of 70th Sentai Ki-44-IIbs using a Toyota KC truck. The shaft above the cab of the vehicle was connected to the lug on the aircraft's spinner in order to start the fighter's Ha-109 engine. These trucks were used to start many different IJAAF aircraft types, and they were a common sight on airfields. Aircraft "12" and "63" show evidence of former ownership by 47th Sentai, having probably been relinquished when that unit began to re-equip with the Ki-84 Hayate. (Tony Holmes Collection)

propeller and two more mounted in the wings. This should have been sufficient firepower for fighter-versus-fighter combat, but by war's end VII Fighter Command pilots had claimed more Shokis destroyed than any other IJAAF fighter.

Ki-61-I KAIc HEIN ("TONY")

The handsome lines of the Kawasaki Ki-61 resembled those of early-model P-51s, but by the time Heins and Mustangs met in the skies over Japan, the American fighter's performance had advanced well beyond that of the Ki-61-I KAIc.

The Hein was a low-wing, single-seat fighter with an all-metal, oval-section fuselage measuring 29ft 4in. in length – about eight inches longer than previous models. Its wing, of 39ft 4.5in. in span, had three spars and split flaps, and the control surfaces were fabric-covered. The main landing gear folded inward, and the tailwheel was fixed. As the first Japanese fighter with protection from enemy gunfire built in, the Ki-61 had self-sealing wing and fuselage fuel tanks (total capacity 145.3 gallons), armored glass in the windscreen, and 13mm steel armor for the pilot's head and back. Its takeoff weight was 7,650lb.

Groundcrew wave farewell to a Ki-61-I KAIc of 244th Sentai HQ Shotai second element as it taxies out for takeoff. "52," probably flown by Lt Itakura, appears to have had its wing-mounted Type 1 (Ho-103) machine guns removed in order to lighten the fighter in an attempt to improve its performance in combat over the Home Islands. (Tony Holmes Collection)

Ki-61-la ARMAMENT

Initially, the Hien was lightly armed, with the Ki-61-la depicted here featuring just two Type 89 7.7mm guns in the wings and two Type 1 (Ho-103) 12.7mm weapons mounted above the engine. Rate of fire for the Type 1 was 750 rounds per minute, and the Ki-61-la carried 250 rounds for each gun. The Ki-61-lb was later up-gunned to carry four 12.7mm machine guns, while 388 Ki-61-las and -lbs were modified on the assembly line through the fitment of a single Mauser MG 151 20mm cannon per wing – each gun could fire 120 rounds. By war's end the Ki-61-ll KAlb was armed with four Ho-5 20mm cannon, this weapon boasting an impressive firing rate of 850 rounds per minute.

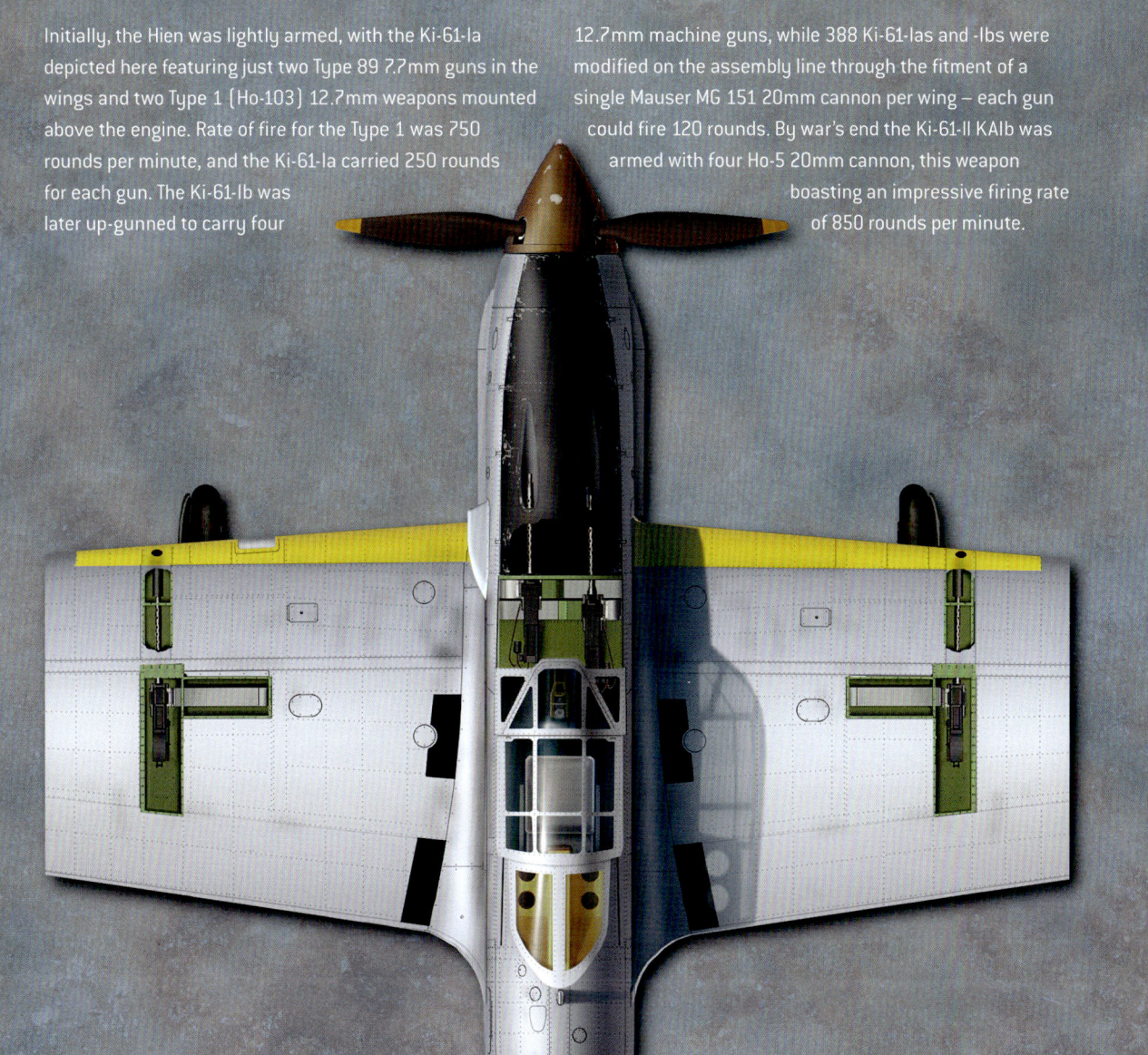

The powerplant in the Ki-61-I KAIc was a liquid-cooled Kawasaki Ha-40 inverted V12, built under license from Daimler-Benz in Germany. The engine produced 1,100hp at 12,800ft. It drove a constant-speed, three-bladed propeller measuring 8ft 10in. in diameter. The aircraft's radiator, like the Mustang's, was mounted under the fuselage near the center of gravity. The Ki-61-I KAIc was well armed, boasting two 20mm Ho-5 cannon with 120 rounds per gun in the forward fuselage firing through the propeller arc and two 12.7 mm Type 1 (Ho-103) machine guns with 200 rounds per weapon in the wings.

Top speed of the Ki-61-I KAIc was 366mph at 13,980ft, and its service ceiling was 32,100ft. The aircraft could climb to 16,405ft in seven minutes.

With 1,274 built between January 1944 and January 1945, the Ki-61-I KAIc was the most numerous variant of the Hein that fought Mustangs over Japan.

Ki-100-I

As the re-engined progeny of Kawasaki's Ki-61-II KAI Hein, the Ki-100 shared many specifications with the previous design. Both aircraft had the same wing design as the Ki-61-I, and the fuselages of the first 274 Ki-100-Is were identical to the Ki-61-II KAI from the firewall back. The final 99 Ki-100-Ibs featured a new canopy with improved vision from the cockpit and a cut-down rear dorsal fuselage.

With its stubby nose mounting the 1,500hp Mitsubishi Ha-112-II Ru 14-cylinder radial engine, the Ki-100 fuselage, measuring 28ft 11.5in., was a foot shorter than the Ki-61-II. Its wingspan was 39ft 4.5in. and the maximum takeoff weight, at 7,705lb (Ki-100-I), was some 700lb lighter than the Ki-61-II. Furthermore, since the air-cooled engine of the Ki-100 did not require the mounting of a radiator, the aircraft suffered little if any penalty in streamlining despite its blunt nose.

When IJAAF pilots first got their hands on the Ki-100, they were delighted by its speed (367mph at 19,685ft), climb rate of 1,604ft per minute, and service ceiling of 37,729ft. Maneuverability was considered to be excellent, and the Ki-100's armament of two Ho-5 20mm cannons in the wings and two Type 1 (Ho-103) 12.7mm machine guns in the fuselage was more than adequate to bring down any Allied fighter.

Despite its sterling qualities as a weapon of war, the Ki-100 was a classic case of "too little, too late." With fewer than 400 examples completed between March 1945 and the end of hostilities, the Ki-100 was little more than an intriguing fortuity that had no bearing on the outcome of the air war over Japan.

5th Sentai Ki-100-Ibs being prepared for flight at Kiyoso. Note the worn cowling on the aircraft in the background. The Ki-100 was never allocated an Allied reporting name, usually being identified in combat by opposing pilots as a Ki-84 "Frank" or A6M Zero-sen. (Tony Holmes Collection)

Ki-84-I HAYATE ("FRANK")

One IJAAF fighter that might have made a difference in the aerial battles over Japan in 1945 was the Nakajima Ki-84, but unrelenting problems with its Nakajima Ha-45 engine hampered the effectiveness of this otherwise outstanding design throughout its brief service life. The 18-cylinder radial engine packed a hefty 1,900hp into a small-diameter package, giving Nakajima designers the opportunity to pen a sleek fuselage that helped to produce the highest top speed (392mph at 20,080ft) of any operational Japanese fighter in World War II. The aircraft's maneuverability was also considered to be excellent by those who flew it.

In common with other Japanese mid-war fighter designs, the Ki-84 was a low-wing, single-seat monoplane of all-metal construction and fabric-covered control surfaces. It was equipped with all the expected features, including cockpit armor, self-sealing fuel tanks, and a full-vision sliding canopy. The pilot could opt for full flaps when landing or 15-degree opening to improve maneuverability in close combat situations. The internal fuel capacity of 162 gallons yielded a combat range of just over 1,000 miles. Wing racks could be fitted with drop tanks to extend range or two 550lb bombs for ground attack, although neither of these options came into play when Ki-84s were undertaking defensive duties over central Japan.

The Ki-84 shared a similar armament suite with several other Japanese fighters, namely two Type 1 (Ho-103) 12.7mm machine guns with 350 rounds per gun in the nose and two Ho-5 20mm cannon with 150 rounds per gun in the wings. One shortcoming of the Ki-84, in addition to its unreliable engine, was its weak main landing gear. Both problems were exacerbated by the considerable number of undertrained IJAAF fighter pilots who were trying to tame the high-performance Ki-84 in the closing months of the war.

With flaps extended, a Ki-84-I Hayate of 11th Sentai's 1st Chutai lands at Takahagi, in the Kanto Region. 11th Sentai converted from Ki-43s to Ki-84s in March 1944 at Tokorozawa, flying the Hayate through to war's end. All of its fighters were marked with a lightning bolt on the tail, with white for 1st Chutai aircraft, red for 2nd Chutai, and yellow for 3rd Chutai. (Peter M. Bowers Collection/Museum of Flight)

THE STRATEGIC SITUATION

Japan had already lost its war against the Western Allies when P-51D Mustangs of VII Fighter Command flew their first combat mission over Tokyo on April 7, 1945, but the Imperial Supreme War Command was not willing to accept the inevitable just yet. It would take four more months of grueling air combat, followed by two explosions more destructive than anything the world had seen before, to seal the deal.

The fortunes of war started turning against Japan in the summer of 1942, when the successful American landings on Guadalcanal, in the Solomon Islands, marked the end of Japanese expansion in the South Pacific. In just six months, Japan had gobbled up the resource-rich areas of its so-called Greater East Asia Co-Prosperity Sphere and then began devoting those resources in petroleum, minerals, and rubber to its war effort. Now the challenge for Japan would be to maintain control of those areas – a challenge it ultimately proved unable to meet. While the Allies were holding the line in India and those parts of China not under Japanese control, their forces chipped away at the enemy's conquered territories in the Pacific. By mid-1944, they were preparing to take the fight to Japan's Home Islands.

At the beginning of the war, Japan's plan for defending the Home Islands presumed that distance would be the primary weapon. With eastern China already subdued, the Imperial Japanese Army would capture territories in the Central and South Pacific to deny the enemy bases within range of Japan, while the Imperial Japanese Navy (IJN) attained control of the seas to keep Allied naval forces at bay.

The first indication that this strategy was insufficient came on April 18, 1942, when 16 B-25 bombers led by Lt Col Jimmy Doolittle performed a surprise attack on

B-29 42-24494 *Mary Ann* of the 792nd BS/468th BG releases its load of AN-M64 500lb high-explosive bombs on Hatto, Formosa, on October 18, 1944. The AN-M64 was the standard general purpose (GP) bomb carried by the B-29, with between 50–55 percent of the weapon's weight being high explosive. *Mary Ann* overshot the runway on 17 June, 1945, and was written off. (National Museum of the USAF)

Tokyo after taking off from the aircraft carrier USS *Hornet* (CV-8). A much more serious blow came six weeks later when the US Navy prevailed at the Battle of Midway, the IJN losing four aircraft carriers, one cruiser, approximately 3,000 men, and hundreds of aircraft. As a result, Japanese expansion in the Pacific would be reversed and the IJN was permanently weakened.

The Imperial Supreme War Command set about stiffening the air defenses of the Home Islands. The nation was divided into air defense regions, with IJAAF and IJNAF units sharing responsibilities within these areas. Frontline fighters replaced obsolete IJAAF Ki-27 "Nates" and IJNAF A5M "Claudes" previously charged with protecting Japan, and the number of units devoted to air defense grew.

From mid-1944, the Japanese encountered a new challenge when long-ranging USAAF B-29 Superfortresses started attacking targets in Manchuria and Kyushu from bases in China. Seeing the threat these high-flying behemoths posed, Japanese air defense units began concentrating their training programs on tactics for opposing them.

Meanwhile, US forces had invaded the Mariana Islands, some 1,500 miles south of Tokyo, in order to build air bases from which the B-29s would be able to attack the Japanese capital and nearby industrial centers in Nagoya, Osaka, and Kobe.

The Kanto Region, which covered the industrial and population centers in and around Tokyo, Yokohama, and Kawasaki, had the highest defense priority. Units protecting these areas were the IJAAF's 10th Shidan (Flying Division) and the IJNAF's 302nd Kokutai, supplemented in February 1945 by 601st Kokutai. In the Central Region, defending Nagoya, Osaka, and Kobe just to the south, were the IJAAF's 11th Shidan and two IJNAF Kokutai, 210th at Nagoya and 332nd at Osaka/Kobe.

These two regions would bear the brunt of the B-29 attacks from November 1944, and they would see all the fighter-versus-fighter combat against VII Fighter Command when the Iwo Jima-based P-51Ds commenced operations in April 1945. A third

This map shows the locations of
the fighter bases used by IJAAF
and the IJNAF units tasked with
defending Tokyo Bay during 1945.

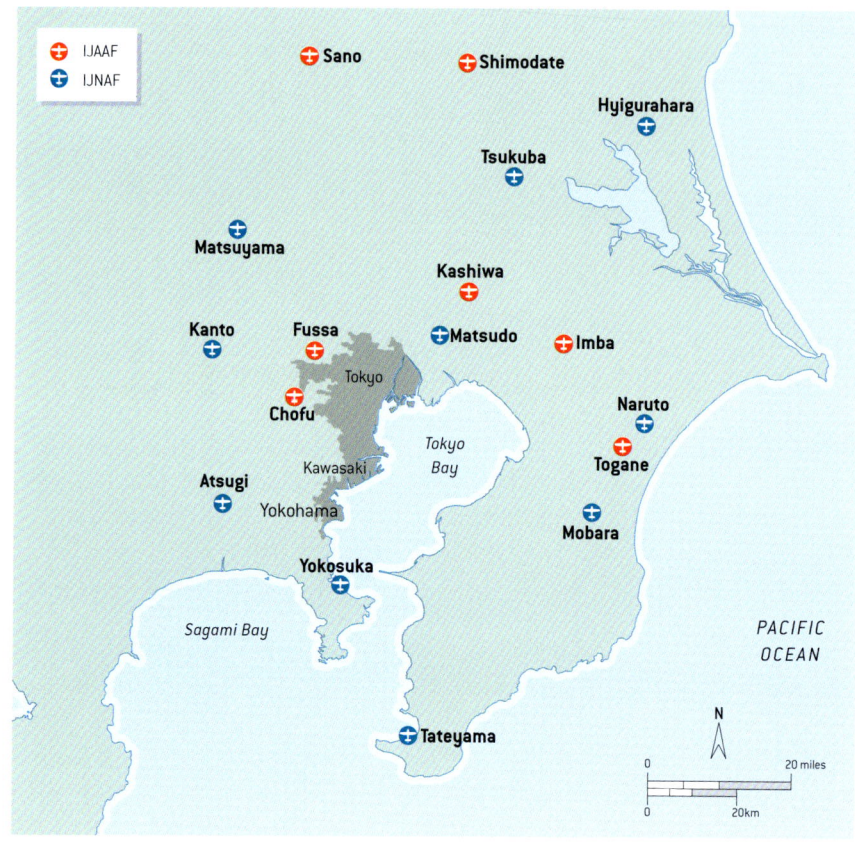

region, the Eastern, defended southern Japan, including Kyushu, but it was beyond the effective range of Iwo Jima-based Mustangs.

At the time of the Doolittle Raid, just 244th Sentai defended the Kanto Region with 50 Ki-27 "Nate" fighters and a handful of Ki-61 prototypes. By July 1944, 10th Shidan had grown in size to five Sentai and one Dokoritu Chutai (Independent Reconnaissance Squadron) totaling around 200 aircraft. Of these units, 47th Sentai (Ki-44s) was considered most competent, followed by 244th Sentai (Ki-61s). 18th Sentai (Ki-61s), 23rd Sentai (Ki-43s), and 53rd Sentai (Ki-45s) were still considered below standard in October. In November 1944, the IJNAF's 302nd Kokutai had a force of 40 J2M Raidens, 38 A6M5 Zero-sen, and 48 nightfighters of several types on hand in the Kanto Region.

Defending the Central Region would be more difficult due to its topography, including a complex coastline and a mountain range running through the middle of the territory. 11th Shidan, formed in July 1944, initially had three Sentai – 55th and 56th, both equipped with Ki-61s, and 246th, flying Ki-44s. All three of these units were transferred elsewhere in the fall of 1944 to respond to Allied air attacks in the Philippines, Formosa, and on Kyushu, although they returned to the Central Region in 1945.

The IJNAF's contribution to the Central Region air defense was a mixed force of J2Ms, N1K2s, A6M5s, and nightfighters totaling about 130 aircraft of 332nd and 210th Kokutai.

Air raid warning systems in the Kanto and Central regions consisted of lookouts, picket boats, radar stations, and radio intercept posts. Minimal resources were allotted to them early in the war, but they were built up quickly once it became clear in 1944 that these two regions would soon be subjected to attacks from both B-29s and carrier-based naval aircraft.

Lookout posts were established throughout each region, with a combination of military and civilian staffers manning them. They fed information on aircraft sightings by landlines to an area headquarters, which served as a clearing house for passing warnings up the chain of command to the Shidan and Kokutai. Initially, such information was unreliable due to the sky watchers' lack of skills and inadequate equipment. Training in aircraft identification and altitude estimation helped, along with improved binoculars, and by the end of 1944 reports were considered more accurate and dependable.

Eventually, 76 military-staffed and 208 civilian lookout posts were operating in the Kanto Region alone. Numerous sites were established in the Central Region as well, but their sighting reports were found to be more useful for 10th Shidan in the Kanto Region because of the diversionary tactics developed by the Americans to confuse Japanese lookouts.

Picket boats equipped with radios, but not radar, patrolled the seas east and southeast of Japan. Initially, they formed a line 600 miles offshore from the Home Islands, but heavy losses to US Navy vessels and air attacks forced them to move closer to land (and farther from the enemy), reducing the usefulness of the information they sent. In November 1944, two radar-equipped picket boats were stationed 200 miles offshore, but only one of them was operational due to malfunctioning equipment onboard the other vessel. With the sinking of the functioning boat in March 1945, the IJN was left with no radar-equipped picket boats by the time VLR Mustangs began operating from Iwo Jima.

Hiens of 244th Sentai fly a patrol over Tokyo Bay, the aircraft being led by Capt Fumisuke Shono in a Mauser MG 151/20-armed Ki-61-Ib – the weapons' barrels can be seen protruding from the wing leading edges. 244th was the first Sentai assigned to Japan strictly for air defense duties. Commanded by noted ace Maj Teruhiko Kobayashi, the unit flew Ki-61s until converting to Ki-100s in the last months of the war. (Tony Holmes Collection)

IMPERIAL
PALACE

TOKYO

FUNABASHI

CHIBA

YOKOHAMA

TOKYO BAY

KIZARAZU

YOKOSUKA
NAVAL BASE

FUTTSU

Seen from the south, this illustration of Tokyo Bay depicts a view that became familiar to pilots of VII Fighter Command after their first VLR Long Range mission on April 7, 1945. With the completion of just a single mission to the city, pilots were considered members of "The Tokyo Club." (Author's Collection)

Special intelligence units monitoring Allied communications were important because they provided early warning of enemy air attacks. Operators proficient in English and cryptoanalysis monitored and deciphered radio traffic – especially on Saipan and Tinian – to predict when large-scale B-29 operations were about to take place. Central Region radio operators could also monitor transmissions between enemy aircraft in flight to predict air raids. Typically, they were not able to determine the bombers' routes or their targets, however. Radar was better for doing that.

As late as 1941, the only radar operated by the Japanese was the Type A fixed-beam vertical scanner. Available in units ranging in strength from three watts to 400 watts, Type A could only see in one direction on a narrow vertical plain. Sites were set up to provide what might be described as electronic "trip wires" ringing each of the air defense regions. Of necessity, the beams only covered land territory, and so had no early-warning capability.

Much-improved Type B radar, developed by the Tama Army Technical Research Station, was deployed shortly after Doolittle's Tokyo raid. It had a range of 125 to 150 miles and the ability to scan in a 90-degree arc to provide region coverage. The IJAAF's seven locations along the Kanto Region coastline and on Hachijajima Island provided overlapping coverage of the approaches that raiding American aircraft were likely to take. The effectiveness of the radar system grew with experience and training so that by late November 1944 its operators were able to identify incoming B-29s and predict their altitude and speed.

Radar was much less effective in the Central Region due to the difficulty in locating station sites where the radar beams would not be blocked by nearby terrain. The latter meant that radar stations were also too far apart to allow for overlapping coverage. They had particular trouble spotting fighters and other smaller aircraft. According to one post-war assessment based on Japanese records, "No information concerning the enemy's frequent raids from Iwo Jima and Okinawa or from carrier task forces was ever available to 11th Shidan prior to the time of the actual appearance of the planes over

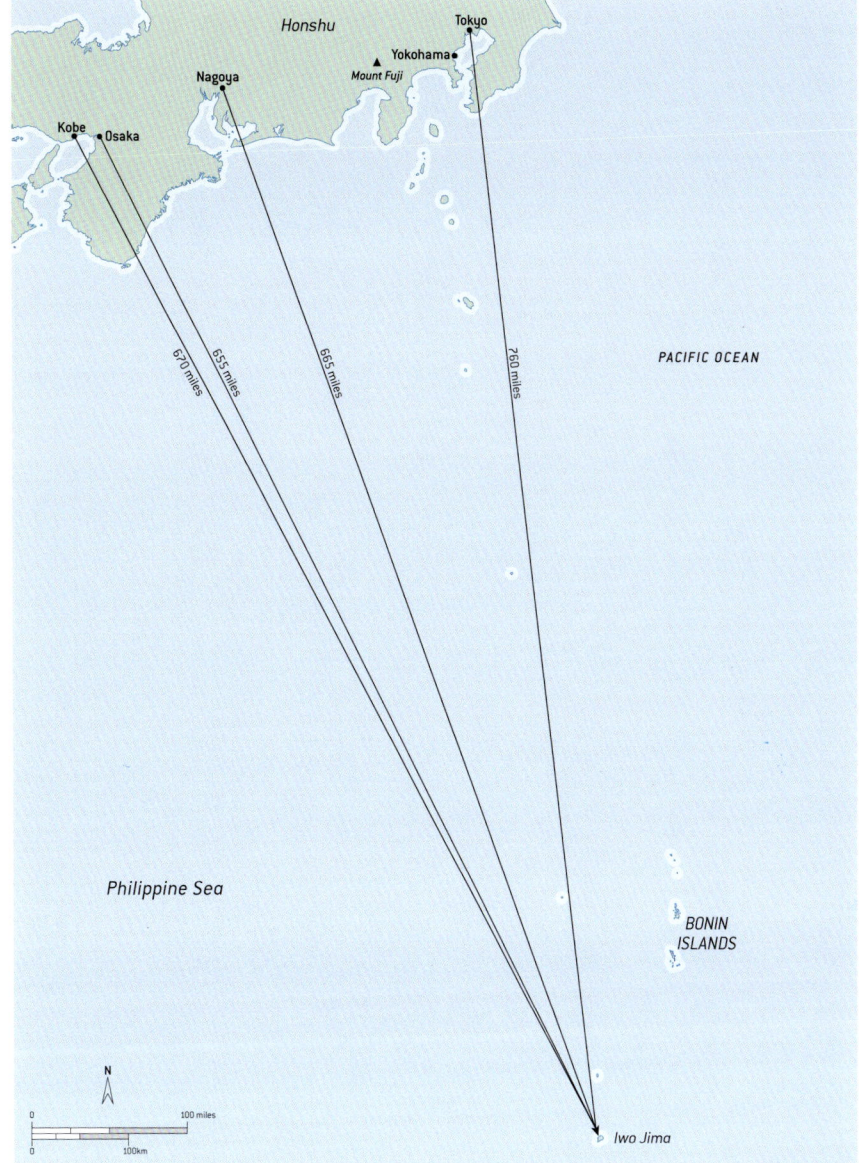

Honshu
Tokyo
Yokohama
Nagoya
▲ Mount Fuji
Kobe
Osaka

670 miles
655 miles
665 miles
260 miles

PACIFIC OCEAN

Philippine Sea

BONIN
ISLANDS

N

0   100 miles
0   100km

Iwo Jima

This map graphically illustrates the huge distances flown by Iwo Jima-based P-51D Mustang units of VII Fighter Command tasked with escorting B-29s targeting the Japanese Home Islands.

the Central Region." When the capture of Iwo Jima by US forces allowed the deployment of P-51Ds to escort the B-29s operating from the Mariana Islands, "the air defenses of Japan were all but helpless to defend the Central Region."

Information from all these sources flowed upward to 10th and 11th Shidan operations rooms, which directed all air defense combat for their respective regions. These rooms operated in three eight-hour shifts per day, but all personnel were called in when an attack was underway. A large information board showed positions of enemy formations, and a weather chart indicated flying conditions and visibility. From the operations room, radio and direct telephone lines maintained communications with subordinate IJAAF units, while air-to-ground radio telephones enabled the operations room to keep in touch with friendly fighters in the air.

The IJNAF constructed its own radar systems in the Kanto and Central regions, as well as in its primary air defense area, Kyushu's Western Region. This wasteful duplication of resources was a product of the intractable IJA–IJN rivalry that hampered Japan's military effectiveness throughout the war. Air raid information was shared between IJAAF and IJNAF fighter director centers, but that was the extent of the cooperation. In keeping with long-established tradition, the rival services each made their own decisions about which units to scramble when, and where to send them.

AMERICAN BUILD-UP

While the Japanese were making their belated effort to shore up air defenses over the Home Islands, the Americans proceeded boldly to prepare for their final aerial offensive of World War II. The first plan was to bomb Japan with the new B-29 Superfortress from bases in central China. There were several problems with this approach, however. Not only were the logistics required to support B-29 operations in remote China daunting, but also the bases were too far west for the bombers to reach beyond Kyushu, southernmost of Japan's Home Islands.

While the first B-29 missions were getting underway from China, American invasion forces went ashore in the Mariana Islands with the objective of moving the Twentieth Air Force's B-29s to new bases on Saipan, Tinian, and Guam, just 1,500 miles south of Tokyo. On November 24, 1944, 111 B-29s made their first attack on Tokyo when they bombed the Musashino aircraft plant and various secondary targets. One bomber was brought down by a ramming fighter and a second B-29 ditched en route home due to fuel exhaustion.

In keeping with pre-war American bombing philosophy, it was assumed that the B-29s would fly high and fast enough, carrying heavy defensive armament, to conduct their attacks without the need for protection from escort fighters. In February 1945

On February 19, 1945, the US Marine Corps' V Amphibious Corps landed three Marine divisions on Iwo Jima, in the Bonin Islands, with the primary goal of securing a base for VLR P-51D operations over Japan. The ground echelon of the 15th FG landed less than a week after the invasion began, commencing the construction of a rudimentary air base. (Author's Collection)

American forces invaded Iwo Jima, in the Bonin Islands, some 760 miles south of Tokyo. Now the American bombers would have an option for landing short of the Marianas should they suffer battle damage or fuel starvation. In addition, there would be room on Iwo Jima to build airfields for three P-51D fighter groups (and later a fourth P-47N-equipped group) of VII Fighter Command to provide escort for the B-29s.

As early as July 1944, Maj Gen Henry "Hap" Arnold, Commanding General of the USAAF, had recommended that VII Fighter Command should be based on Iwo Jima for long-range operations against Japan. That decision began coming to life in September when Brig Gen Ernest "Mickey" Moore, commanding officer of VII Fighter Command, traveled from his headquarters in Hawaii to England so he could pick the brains of Eighth Air Force fighter commanders about the finer points of long-range escort operations.

Brig Gen Ernest "Mickey" Moore, a graduate of the US Military Academy at West Point, New York, was the commanding officer of VII Fighter Command. He was promoted from executive officer of the unit in November 1944, and remained in command throughout the VLR campaign. Moore retired from the USAF with the rank of major general in 1961. (Author's Collection)

Moore was particularly eager to learn all he could about the newest fighter in the USAAF arsenal, the P-51 Mustang, which had been battling the Luftwaffe over occupied Europe with great success since December 1943. Not long after he returned to Hawaii, the first shipment of brand-new P-51D-20s began arriving at Hickam Air Depot, on Oahu, nearly two months before the invasion of Iwo Jima.

One runway already existed on Iwo Jima when the US Marine Corps landed there on February 19, 1945, and engineers immediately got to work building three more. This was no small task, considering Japanese soldiers were still fighting on the island, and the size of Iwo Jima – five miles long and eight square miles area – made it a tight squeeze to fit in all the facilities. Fortunately, the terrain allowed all the runways to be parallel, running east–west. Rebuilding the southernmost airfield was completed while the engineers were still under fire.

Ground personnel of the first two USAAF fighter groups (the 15th and 21st FGs) assigned to Iwo Jima, began arriving on February 25, 1945. Both had been based in Hawaii for more than a year, transitioning to Mustangs in December 1944. Many of the pilots had gained combat experience during Operation *Flintlock* (the Gilbert and Marshall Islands campaign) in the Central Pacific from the fall of 1943 through to February 1944, flying P-39s and P-40s. The 506th FG arrived in late April from Florida, where it had been working up on Mustangs since the previous October. The officers in most of its leadership roles had spent long months as Army Air Forces

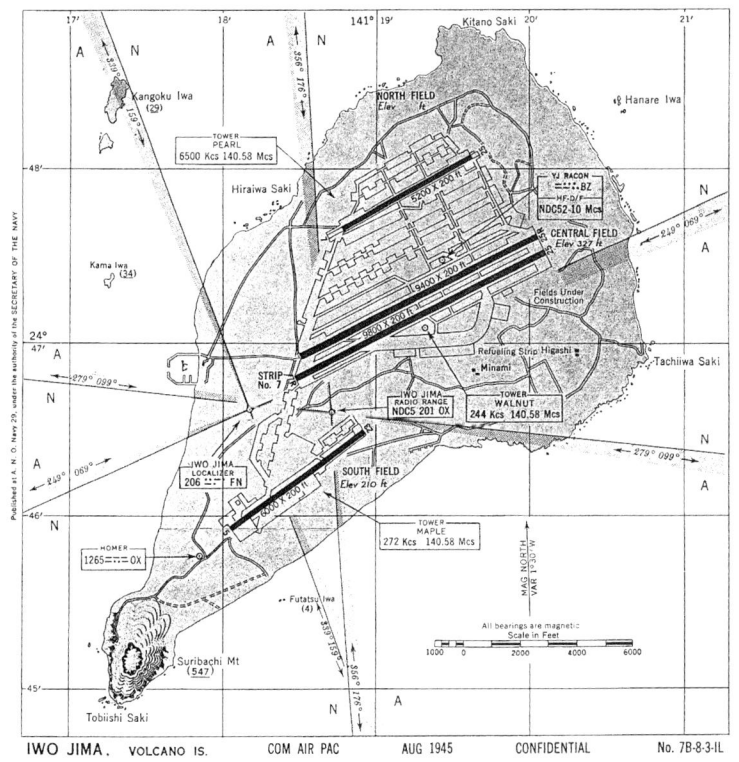

This map of Iwo Jima (which was about six miles long and two miles wide) was produced by the US Navy in the final weeks of World War II. The four runways that turned the island into an "unsinkable aircraft carrier" are clearly marked. Mount Suribachi, at the southwestern tip of Iwo Jima, was an extinct volcano. (Author's Collection)

Training Command instructors before joining the 506th, and they were eager to exploit their many hours of flight experience in a combat environment.

On March 6, 1945, South Field on Iwo Jima was declared ready for operations, and Brig Gen Moore led the first 25 Mustangs to the embattled island that same day. Conditions there were a rude change for the men of VII Fighter Command, who had spent so many months in the pleasant surroundings of Hawaii. 1Lt Charles Butler was one of the pilots who flew in on the second day. He recalled:

> On arrival on Iwo, I was surprised by the lack of vegetation, which had been destroyed by air bombing, heavy offshore naval fire, ground fire, and the creation of dugouts, built mostly by the Japs. Many dead Japs had been quickly buried and only partially covered, and some were still exposed.

Combat operations began on March 8, 1945, when two flights of P-51s flew a strafing mission against stubborn Japanese positions on the north coast of Iwo Jima. Three days later, 17 pilots flew VII Fighter Command's first overwater mission – a strike against the Japanese-held island of Chichi Jima, 150 miles north of Iwo and a key listening post in the enemy's air-defense system. The first Mustang mission over Japan proper was only three weeks away.

P-51D-20 44-63465 "56" of the 45th FS was one of 82 Mustangs from the 15th FG shipped to the Mariana Islands from Hawaii aboard the aircraft carrier USS *Sitkoh Bay* (CVE-86) in early February 1945. The aircraft is seen here being lightered ashore to Guam after being craned off the carrier, the fighter subsequently being flown to Tinian and then on to Iwo Jima. (Author's Collection)

Col James O. Beckwith, CO of the 15th FG, leads P-51Ds of the 45th and 78th FSs past Mount Suribachi at the southwestern tip of Iwo Jima on March 10, 1945. This photograph was taken at the end of the ferry flight from Tinian. (Author's Collection)

One of the more effective air defense systems operated by the Japanese consisted of listening posts monitoring American radio transmissions for indications of upcoming raids on the Home Islands. The radio station (center) on Chichi Jima, an island about 150 miles north of Iwo Jima, was attacked regularly by Mustangs of VII Fighter Command. (Author's Collection)

THE COMBATANTS

The US and Japan were two vastly different places in the 1930s and 1940s, each with cultures and traditions that were nearly incomprehensible to the other. The US was a young democracy, not yet 200 years old, founded on the principles of "life, liberty, and the pursuit of happiness." Japan, meanwhile, was an ancient land bound in a strict class structure and ruled by its military. It was only natural that the young men of these two nations would approach military service with different mindsets, although they certainly shared patriotic dedication to their respective homelands.

PILOT TRAINING

Many young men who served in the military during World War II were attracted to the flying services thanks at least in part to the heroic portrayals of World War I flying aces and subsequent aerial adventurers such as Charles Lindbergh and Jimmy Doolittle. This was true the world over, and thus the air forces of Japan and the US were able to set lofty standards for intelligence and physical condition in their pilot recruits.

The training programs established in both countries were similar in structure, as might be expected. After all, aircraft operated pretty much the same the world over – control column to the left or right for the ailerons and forward–back for the elevators, rudder pedals for direction, throttle to control engine speed, and flaps to slow down. Two sets of instruments – one to check the mechanical functions and the other to monitor the aircraft's flight. The flight training process started low and slow, before progressing to aircraft with better performance. Once pilots had mastered flying, they moved on to learning how to fight using the aircraft as their weapon.

The massive scope of the USAAF's pilot training effort is obvious in this shot of BT-13 basic trainers on a training airfield in Texas just before the start of the Pacific War. Pilots earned an officer's commission and their wings after about nine months of instruction and 200 hours of flight time. (Author's Collection)

Training started with general military instruction, which could last several months, and then student pilots began flying lessons in primary school on docile training aircraft. The USAAF's primary trainers were the Stearman PT-17 biplane and the Ryan PT-21/22, an open-cockpit monoplane. The Tachikawa Ki-17 "Cedar" was the IJAAF's primary trainer, while the IJNAF initially used the Yokosuka K2Y2 until it was replaced by the Watanabe K9W1 "Cypress" (license-built Bücker Bü 131 Jungmann) from the fall of 1942 – all three aircraft were biplanes.

One of the main purposes of primary training was to weed out those who showed no talent for flying. The students who qualified moved on to the next level, called "basic training" by the USAAF and IJNAF, but "advanced training" in the IJAAF. USAAF basic students flew the North American BT-9 and Vultee BT-13/15, both

IJAAF trainee pilots learned to fly in the Ki-9 "Spruce," which was used as a primary trainer throughout the Pacific War. More than 2,600 examples were built, with the aircraft remaining in production for the best part of a decade. (Tony Holmes Collection)

fixed-gear, low-wing monoplanes with enclosed canopies over their two cockpits. The Japanese stuck to biplane trainers at this stage, namely the Tachikawa Ki-9 "Spruce" for the IJAAF and Yokosuka K5Y1/2 "Willow" for the IJNAF.

USAAF pilots selected for single-engined duties at the end of basic training moved up to the NAA AT-6 Texan for advanced training. Similar in layout to the BT-9, the AT-6 featured a more powerful engine, retractable landing gear, and a single 0.30-cal. machine gun in the nose for gunnery instruction. The IJAAF termed its last phase of general instruction as operational training, taught at the controls of a Tachikawa Ki-55 "Ida" two-seat, low-wing monoplane with fixed landing gear that was also used for IJA cooperation duties. IJNAF cadets flew older, obsolete service types, such as surplus A5M "Claude" fighters (and a small number of A5M4-K two-seaters), for their operational training.

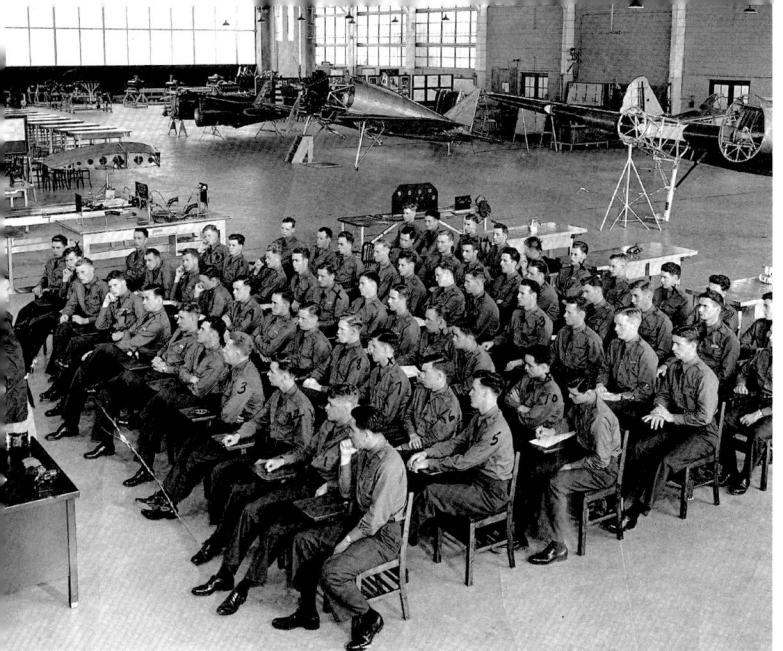

Trainee pilots of the USAAF faced long hours of classroom study in addition to their flight training before they could qualify for their wings. Here, cadets in Class 40F attend a basic training lecture in a hangar at Randolph Field, Texas. (Author's Collection)

Although both nations used a three-phase structure for flight training, there were three significant differences in their programs. The first was flight time, which increasingly diverged as the war progressed. An American pilot would receive his wings and officer's commission after about nine months of instruction and 200 hours of flight time. During the pre-war years, he would then be assigned to an active squadron, where his flying skills would continue to develop while flying frontline combat aircraft.

In December 1942, the USAAF instituted Fighter Replacement Training Units (FRTUs) to give newly minted fighter pilots further training in the types of aircraft they could expect to be flying in combat. The FRTU courses (normally about two months in duration) included instrument training and night flying, air-to-air and air-to-ground gunnery instruction, and practice in formation flying and combat maneuvering.

IJAAF fighter pilots who completed operational training were assigned to a Kyoiku Hikotai (flying training unit) for six months. Then they were posted to a fighter Sentai, where they undertook an additional three months of training prior to entering combat. New IJNAF pilots were assigned to a specific aircraft type in an operational unit after advanced training. Often these were new units in the process of forming, which gave the fledgling pilots time (about 150 hours) to hone their combat skills prior to flying their first operational missions.

Through the early part of the war, Japanese pilots of both services could expect to enter combat with more flight time than their American counterparts. Unlike in the US services, most Japanese pilots began their flying careers as enlisted men rather than junior officers.

The balance in flight training would tip dramatically in favor of US pilots once the war got underway. The Americans held tight to their 200-hour syllabus throughout the conflict, considering this the minimum amount of training needed for a military pilot to attain his wings. But the Japanese did not have this luxury. After the Allies began to gain the upper hand in the Pacific in mid-1942, the Japanese found it increasingly difficult to maintain the quality of their flight instruction due to shortages of fuel and equipment, plus the unforeseen demand for replacement pilots on the war fronts. By 1944, fledgling IJAAF pilots were being sent into combat with a pathetic 60 to 70 hours of flight experience, and the results were predictable.

The respective cultures of the warring nations also had an effect on how their pilots were treated during training. A striking difference was the intensity and methods of imposing discipline on their flight cadets. Both nations recognized the need to establish military order and teach respect for the chain of command among their pilots, but they diverged in the methods of doing so.

The USAAF took a relatively casual approach to training, with classroom instruction on military conduct supplemented by mostly gentle "hazing" from training instructors and senior cadets. Punishments for infractions – forgetting to salute a superior or failing an inspection, for instance – were likely to be assignments to some of the more unsavory tasks connected with military service, such as guard duty and kitchen clean-up. Since the goal of student pilots was to graduate from flight school and become a military pilot, the threat of expulsion was all the motivation most cadets needed to learn the rules and obey them.

Japanese military training was altogether different in this regard. Its top priority was to instill total dedication to Emperor Hirohito and to Japan in its fighting men, along with complete disregard for one's self-interest. As had been the case for centuries, the Japanese were taught that they would gain the greatest honor by dying for their country, with a complete disdain for suffering, surrender, or death. A key element in teaching this to young men, mostly in their teens, was corporal punishment. IJAAF pilot Yasuo Kuwahara described his thoughts on this topic in his book, *Kamikaze*:

Military men, regardless of nationality, follow the same basic rules. The great difference lay in how these rules were enforced. An American, for example, who failed to be clean shaven or to have his shoes properly shined for an inspection, might have his pass revoked for a day or two, or he might be given extra guard duty. For us, however, as for all of Nippon's basic trainees, the slightest infraction, the most infinitesimal mistake, brought excruciating punishment.

What I can only describe as a siege of ruthless discipline and relentless castigation began in the first hours of our arrival and thereafter never ceased during all the days of our training – a siege so terrible that some did not survive it. No matter how perfectly we performed our tasks, the "hancho" [training instructor] found excuses to make us suffer. Punishment was an integral part of our training and served two main purposes – to create unwavering discipline and to develop an invincible fighting spirit.

For all of us it was a question not merely of learning skills but of survival. Anyone who could withstand the "hancho" would never run from the enemy and would prefer death to surrender. Whether this policy really produced superior fighting men, I am not prepared to say. Courage may have more than one connotation. Nonetheless, it did create men who either were so fearless or so dedicated that they would almost invariably fight to the death.

Ultimately, a substantial proportion of Japanese fighter pilots did in fact fight to the death during World War II, although a quirk of fate saved Kuwahara from being one of them. Another surviving fighter pilot, high-scoring IJNAF ace Saburo Sakai, gave an example of the rigid standards trainees faced in his book, *Samurai*:

No fewer than 5,770 examples of the K5Y1/2 "Willow" intermediate trainer were built between 1933 and 1945. Later in the war, 176 Kyushu K10W1s (licensed-built NAA NA-16 monoplane trainers modified specifically for IJNAF use) supplemented them. (Tony Holmes Collection)

The Ki-55 "Ida" acted as a bridge between the Ki-9 "Spruce" and the more demanding operational fighter aircraft that a young IJAAF pilot would fly in his last stage of training. This photograph shows Ki-55s from Koku Shikan Gakko (Army Air Academy) practicing formation flying. Koku Shikan Gakko exclusively trained officer pilots, with enlisted aviators undertaking a separate training program. (Tony Holmes Collection)

The rigidity of this weeding-out process was forcibly brought home to us on the very eve of our graduation. On that same day, one of the remaining students was expelled. A shore patrol discovered him entering an off-limits bar in the town of Tsuchiura to celebrate his "graduation." He was premature in more respects than one. Upon his return to the billet, he was ordered to report at once to his faculty board. By way of apology the student knelt on the floor before the officers, but to no avail.

The faculty board found him guilty of two unpardonable sins. The first, every pilot knew. That was that a combat pilot shall never, for any reason, drink alcoholic beverages the evening before he flies. As part of the graduation exercises, we were to pass over the field in formation flight the next day. The second of the two crimes was more commonplace, but equally serious. No member of the Navy was ever to disgrace his service by entering any establishment marked "off limits."

The differences in training techniques of the two nations came into play when their fighter pilots encountered each other in combat, to be sure. But ultimately it was the difference in their efforts to address the sheer scope of the training challenge that set them apart. From the beginning, Japanese war planners failed to understand this issue. They assumed the war with the US would be settled quickly with lightning victories throughout the Pacific – a gross miscalculation on their part.

When the IJAAF established the Army Youth Pilot Program in 1938 to begin building up strength for the coming war, its initial intake was just 120 student pilots in two schools. Even in 1941, the IJNAF was turning out just 2,000 new pilots a year. By contrast, in 1939, when the US government sponsored the Civilian Pilot Training Program, the first year goal was to produce 20,000 new pilots. The imbalance grew as the war progressed.

By V-J Day, Japan had produced around 46,000 pilots of all types, while no fewer than 193,440 Americans had earned their wings between 1941 and 1945. From December 1942 through to August 1945, the USAAF graduated 35,000 fighter pilots from its FRTUs alone. Even when considering that US forces was fighting a two-front war while Japan was not, the sheer weight of numbers of American pilots made the outcome of the Pacific air war a foregone conclusion. Nowhere was this more obvious than in the skies over Japan during the closing months of the war.

A contemporary news photograph showing IJAAF fighter pilots at a Kyoiku Hikotai receiving training in air combat maneuvers from their instructor while a Ki-43 flies past overhead. In the early years of the war a great deal of operational training took place at unit level. Some successful pilots who managed to survive combat subsequently returned to Japan to serve as instructors in 1943–44. (Tony Holmes Collection)

ORGANIZATION AND TACTICS

The USAAF and the IJAAF organized their operational combat units similarly. The numbered air forces of the USAAF corresponded to the IJAAF's air armies, each assigned to a specific geographical area. During the final assault on Japan, USAAF fighters on Iwo Jima were under the command of VII Fighter Command, subordinate of the Twentieth Air Force. The IJAAF's air defense force, including 10th (Kanto Region) and 11th (Central Region) Shidan, was unified under a single command, the Koku Sogun (Air General Army), on April 15, 1945. The IJNAF (land-based), meanwhile, maintained a shore-based system of naval air fleets called Koku Kantai.

The basic operational fighter unit in the USAAF was the group, which normally consisted of three squadrons, each divided into four flights. Sixteen fighters made up the standard squadron formation, so a formation at group strength was 48 aircraft. The equivalent of a USAAF group in the IJAAF was termed a Hiko Sentai (usually shortened to Sentai). Typically, a Sentai would consist of two or three Chutai, the equivalent of USAAF squadrons, also comprising 16 aircraft each. A single Chutai contained three flights called Shotai.

In the IJNAF, the basic operational land-based unit was the Kokutai, with about 50 fighters assigned. Up to three subordinate units, called Hikotai, were allocated to a Kokutai, one for each type of aircraft assigned. Hikotai were in turn broken down into Daitai (squadron), Chutai (flight), and Shotai (section). Independent Sento Hikotai began being formed in spring 1944.

In the USAAF, the highest ranking officer flying combat missions was the group commander. In fact one group commander in VII Fighter Command, Lt Col Julian "Jack" Thomas of the 15th FG, was killed in action over Japan.

By 1945, most IJAAF and JNAF fighter units had shifted from obsolete three-aircraft "V" formations to a version of the "finger-four," which the Americans had used so effectively against them. However, the Japanese never seemed to develop the two-fighter section, instead often shifting to attacking in trail when combat was joined.

Many student pilots of the IJNAF received dual instruction in the A6M2-K, a Hitachi-built two-seat version of the Reisen fighter. Two examples, assigned to Genzan Kokutai in Korea, can be seen here having their engines run up alongside A6M2s in April 1945. After mid-1942, the Japanese found it increasingly difficult to maintain the quality of their flight instruction programs. (Author's Collection)

According to historian Richard Dunn:

IJAAF Army Flying Regiments [Sentai] were almost uniformly commanded by experienced flying officers capable of leading them in combat. In the IJNAF both flying officers and non-flying officers commanded Air Groups [Kokutai], and seldom did the CO or even the Executive Officer actually lead the unit in combat. Especially later in the war, the "senior" flying officer was often relatively inexperienced.

By the closing months of the Pacific War, the tactics employed by fighter pilots of both sides were nearly identical. The air forces of the US and Japan had settled on the four-aircraft flight as the most effective formation for combat operations. US units further split flights into two-fighter elements. The line-abreast formation was maneuverable and allowed for mutual support among the pilots. When reforming for dive-bombing or strafing against ground targets, it was a simple matter for the pilots to slip into line astern and follow their leader down. During the campaign over Japan, this tactic applied to the American pilots only, since the Japanese were strictly on the defensive.

All squadrons in VII Fighter Command used the "finger-four" formation, composed of a flight leader with a wingman and an element leader with a wingman. The formation was flexible and effective, the USAAF having adapted it from the Luftwaffe's *Schwarm* (swarm) which resembled four fingers of an outstretched left hand when viewed from above.

Of the Japanese fighter pilots defending the Home Islands, only those flying the A6M Zero-sen retained an advantage in maneuverability over the P-51Ds of VII Fighter Command. But the days of Zero-sen pilots looping up and over or flipping into a tight 360-degree turn to get behind an attacking enemy fighter were over. Allied pilots had long since learned to avoid dogfighting with Japanese fighters, having adopted "dive-and-zoom" tactics that played to their own fighters' strengths.

As we have seen earlier in this book, the later generation of Japanese fighters now in service traded maneuverability for the speed and firepower needed to bring down heavy bombers attacking the homeland. This caused Japanese fighter tactics to evolve, as young pilots were trained to use "dive-and-zoom" attacks that resembled those employed by the Americans.

When it came to fighter-versus-fighter combat over Japan, the old World War I maxim still applied – "Beware of the Hun in the sun." American and Japanese pilots alike were looking to catch their opponent unawares and blast him from the sky before he had a chance to react. Turning combats still occurred, to be sure, but most successful pilots were those who kept their heads swiveling at all times and struck aggressively when an opportunity presented itself.

2Lt Ed Linfante of the 462nd FS/506th FG posed with a P-51C-10 at Lakeland, Florida, in January 1945 while the group was completing its VLR operations training prior to deploying to Iwo Jima. A BT-13 trainer is parked behind the Mustang. (Author's Collection)

CAPT WILLIS E. MATHEWS

Willis Mathews, like many pilots of VII Fighter Command, already had a combat tour and several confirmed victories in his logbook when he flew his first mission over Japan in May 1945.

Mathews was born on November 12, 1920 in the small community of Parkerton, Wyoming. The family moved to Colorado and then California, where he learned to fly during his time at Pasadena Junior College. He joined the Royal Canadian Air Force in Vancouver, British Columbia, on August 6, 1941 as a student pilot, only to be discharged on May 30, 1942 so that he could join the USAAF. Mathews completed pilot training on August 27, 1942 at Victorville, California.

After joining the 84th FS/78th FG at Hamilton Field, California, two months later, Mathews subsequently transferred to the 37th FS/55th FG at Olympia, Washington, from where he flew Lockheed P-38s. Overseas orders sent him to Biskra, Algeria, on January 1, 1943 as a replacement pilot for the 94th FS/1st FG, again flying Lightnings. Mathews already had 222 flight hours of training time and 69.5 hours of fighter time by then. He completed 57 missions and scored 3.5 aerial victories during his Mediterranean tour before returning home in June 1943.

After a short assignment in Ferry Command and nearly two years of instructor duty, Mathews was transferred on May 22, 1945, to VII Fighter Command on Iwo Jima. Assigned to the 531st FS/21st FG, he flew his first mission over Japan on May 25, claiming one aircraft destroyed and three damaged on the ground at Tokorozawa airfield. Mathews' first encounter with Japanese fighters in the air came on June 9, when he scored one A6M or Ki-43 probably destroyed and a Ki-44 damaged over Kagamigahara airfield – the only claims of the day for VII Fighter Command.

A month later, on July 9, Mathews reached ace status when he destroyed a Ki-61 and an A6M over Osaka to bring his score to 5.5 confirmed victories. He also claimed an A6M probable and another damaged on that mission. The Ki-61 kill was unusual, to say the least:

I dropped external tanks and led the squadron down into them. I fired two rockets head-on into the formation, which split them all up. One Tony pulled away straight, and I hit him in the tail with a rocket. A large piece of his tail surface broke off and the rocket exploded directly in front of the enemy. The Tony fell straight down out of control, trailing coolant.

Capt Willis Mathews reached ace status while flying with the 531st FS/21st FG. Here, he is seen posing with a Mustang at Oxnard AFB, California, in 1953. (Author's Collection)

Mathews' final mission was a patrol of the Bonin Islands on August 4, 1945. By then he had amassed an impressive record with VII Fighter Command – two aircraft destroyed and six damaged in the air and two aircraft destroyed, one probable and ten damaged on the ground during the course of 13 missions over Japan. An unfortunate footnote to Mathews' record is that the US Air Force (USAF) did not include his two victories over Japan in its post-war analysis, Historical Study 85, and thus he is not considered an ace by the USAF. Nonetheless, the American Fighter Aces Association accepted him for membership based on the credits listed in the official combat reports of VII Fighter Command.

Mathews became a stockbroker after the war, but he rejoined the USAF when the Korean War started. He flew F-51s and then Lockheed F-94C Starfires in California, returning to his business career in 1953 after that war ended. He died in 2007.

LT(jg) SADAAKI AKAMATSU

Born in 1910 in Kochi Prefecture on Shikoku Island, Sadaaki Akamatsu grew up to become one of Japan's most colorful fighter pilots of World War II. He joined the IJN shortly after his 18th birthday and began flight training two years later, graduating from the arduous program in 1932.

Akamatsu served in several Kokutai, including three assigned to aircraft carriers, during his first five years on flight duties. Five months after Japan went to war with China in July 1937, Akamatsu transferred to 13th Kokutai, flying A5Ms from Shanghai. On February 25, 1938, he claimed four enemy aircraft destroyed over Nanchang in his first aerial combat. Some months later he returned to a hero's welcome in Japan. The boastful Akamatsu proclaimed himself the "King of Aces," but he also gained attention for his heavy drinking and violent displays of temper.

By December 1941 Akamatsu was flying the A6M Zero-sen with the newly reformed 3rd Kokutai at Takao, on Formosa (Taiwan), when war broke out with the US. He claimed several USAAC P-40s shot down over the Philippine Islands in the opening weeks of the conflict, and continued his successes over the Dutch East Indies prior to returning to Japan in May 1942. Akamatsu eventually went back into action with 331st Kokutai in Sumatra, and on December 5, 1943 he claimed five victories during a long escort mission to Calcutta, India.

Again posted back to Japan in early 1944, Akamatsu joined 302nd Kokutai, a newly forming air defense unit equipped with the J2M fighter. His primary job was convincing the 302nd's young pilots that the powerful Raiden, a significant departure from the highly maneuverable A6M, could be an effective fighter if they employed "hit-and-run" tactics against enemy fighters.

Akamatsu's first clash with P-51Ds of VII Fighter Command came on April 19, 1945, when 106 Mustangs attacked Atsugi and Yokosuka airfields. He claimed two or three P-51s destroyed, although only one Mustang was in fact lost that day. Then on May 29, 454 B-29s set out on a fire-bombing raid of Yokohama, with 101 Mustangs of the 15th and 21st FGs as escorts.

Akamatsu, the old master (he was now 35 years old), was able to lead a small force of A6Ms into position above the P-51s before making a slashing solo dive down through them. As he wove his way through the enemy formations, Akamatsu picked out the Mustang flown by 2Lt Rufus Moore of the 45th FS and shot it down in flames, before making his escape. 2Lt Jack

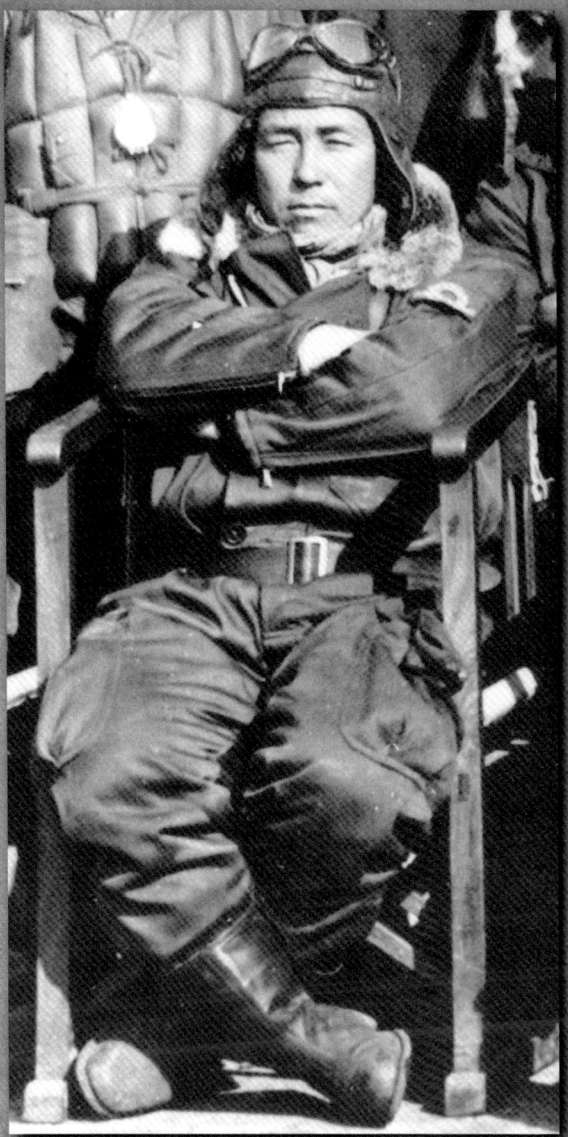

Striking a formidable pose, Lt(jg) Sadaaki Akamatsu was the self-proclaimed "King of Aces" of the IJNAF. (Author's Collection)

Wilson of the 531st FS witnessed Akamatsu's feat, observing later, "He made us look like a bunch of truck drivers."

At war's end, having survived almost four solid years of combat and the earlier fighting in China without ever being wounded, Akamatsu claimed more than 350 aerial victories. It is estimated, however, that his actual tally was closer to 30. The post-war years were not kind to him, and his struggles with alcohol continued unabated. Akamatsu eventually retired to Kochi Prefecture, and he died there of pneumonia in 1980.

COMBAT

By early April 1945, mass formations of B-29s based in the Mariana Islands had been fire-bombing Tokyo at night for several months, laying waste to vast sections of the city. Many key industrial targets that could only be hit by precision daylight bombing remained intact, however. Experience had revealed that bombing accuracy suffered on high-altitude raids because of powerful and unpredictable winds over Japan, but if the B-29s attacked at lower levels they became vulnerable to enemy anti-aircraft fire and fighter interception. Now, with the arrival of Brig Gen "Mickey" Moore's VII Fighter Command Mustangs on Iwo Jima, the bomber crews could expect some protection from Japanese interceptors when they set out for the Home Islands in daylight.

The Americans did not know, however, that the Imperial Supreme War Command was in the process of scaling back its air defense effort. Operation *Ketsu Go* (Decisive), a plan for the all-out defense of Japan against the presumed upcoming Allied invasion, called on IJAAF and IJNAF fighter units to conserve their strength for the final defensive effort. After suffering heavy losses to US Navy Hellcats earlier in the year, Japanese home defense pilots were instructed to avoid combat with enemy fighters except when the defenders had a clear advantage in numbers and/or altitude. Still, interceptions aimed at destroying B-29s would continue, so VII Fighter Command Mustang pilots could expect plenty of action when they began escorting their "Big Friends" to Japan.

APRIL 7, 1945

The Japanese fighter pilots defending Tokyo were in for a surprise on April 7, when they scrambled to oppose what they assumed would be a B-29 raid coming in from the south. The Superfortresses arrived over their target (the Nakajima aircraft engine factories west of the city), but accompanying them for the first time were six squadrons of P-51D escort fighters. And the Mustang pilots were no rookies. To qualify for the mission, each aviator had to show at least 600 flying hours in his logbook.

The Mustangs rendezvoused with the Superfortresses over Kozu-shima, just off the coast of Japan, at 1020 hrs. The bombers flew at 15,000ft, and the fighters fanned out into combat formation several thousand feet above them, with three squadrons of the 21st FG on the left and three more of the 15th FG on the right. The formation hit landfall within ten minutes, and soon Japanese fighters appeared over Sagami-wan between Atami and Hiratsuka, 30 to 45 miles south of the target. The Mustang pilots immediately jettisoned their drop tanks and went to full power, their gunsights switched on.

Confronted by an American force of nearly 200 aircraft, equally divided between B-29s and P-51s, the Japanese pilots did as they had been trained and split up to make individual attacks on the bombers. Blue Flight of the 46th FS/21st FG got the first crack at them when several pilots achieved hits on a Ki-44 Shoki in the vicinity of Yokohama. Within moments, the Mustangs were scrapping with Japanese fighters all over the sky.

One of the IJAAF pilots who succeeded in closing to within firing range of a B-29 was 2Lt Mitsuo Oyake, flying a Ki-61 Hein of 18th Sentai based at Kashiwa. He had reached 29,000ft over the Tama River when he spotted the bomber formation approaching below him. He dove at the Superfortresses, hounded by a P-51 coming in behind him. Oyake eluded the Mustang and picked out a B-29, making several firing runs at it without doing any visible damage. In frustration, he resorted to a taiatari ("body blow") ramming attack and slammed his Hein into the tail section of the bomber. The tail broke away from the B-29, sending it crashing to the ground near the Tokyo suburb of Kugayama. Oyake's crumpled Hein fell in a spiral as the pilot bailed out. He landed unhurt in Sanganjaya, living to fight another day.

The 47th FS/15th FG, led by Capt Robert Down of Green Flight, was the top-scoring Mustang squadron of the day. Down and his element leader, 1Lt Dick Hintermeier, first spotted a Ki-45 over Tokyo Bay at 18,000ft, and both made passes at it before the stricken twin-engined fighter fell away in flames. This was deemed to be the first Japanese aircraft shot down by USAAF fighters over Japan. Down followed it up a few minutes later with a Ki-44.

1Lt Eurich Bright, Down's wingman, attacked a Ki-61 Hein from the rear, setting it on fire. Bright overran his target as it was beginning to break apart, so he pulled up and watched it fall in flames. An A6M Zero-sen then made a pass at Bright, who maneuvered out of the line of fire and latched onto the tail of his opponent as the fighter dove away. Exhibiting the flight discipline learned in long hours of training, Down assumed the role of wingman to Bright and cleared his tail while Bright fired at the fleeing Zero-sen from dead astern. The fighter pulled up, burning, and then fell off in a final dive.

Bright was not finished, however. He then spotted a twin-engined aircraft and shot it down for his third victory of the mission. His last target, another Zero-sen, eluded him in a split-S maneuver, at which point Green Flight called it a day and turned south for the long flight back to Iwo Jima.

Capt Harry Crim (left) of the 531st FS/21st FG, scored the first of his six VLR aerial victories on April 7, 1945. Here, he discusses the mission with Maj DeWitt Spain, deputy commander of the 21st FG, and Brig Gen "Mickey" Moore, CO of VII Fighter Command. (Author's Collection)

Capt Ed Markham was leading Blue Flight of the 47th FS at 17,000ft ahead of the bombers, about 20 miles south of the target, when the Mustang pilots spotted an IJNAF Nakajima C6N Saiun (Painted Cloud) "Myrt" reconnaissance aircraft ahead of them. As the Mustangs closed in, the C6N turned into the path of 1Lt Richard Condrick, Blue Flight element leader, and he fired two bursts into it. The enemy aircraft caught fire and dove away trailing smoke before it was seen to crash into the ground.

At this point, the two Blue Flight elements became separated. Markham headed toward Tokyo and spotted two Ki-45s about 1,000ft below him, heading in the same direction. He closed in behind one of them, gave it a long burst, and was rewarded when the twin-engined aircraft broke up and fell away to earth. Both elements of Blue Flight made several more passes at Japanese fighters without further success before turning for home. The 47th FS's score for the day was seven confirmed victories and two damaged.

On the other side of the B-29s, nine of the 20 Mustangs in the 531st FS/21st FG aborted the mission, leaving unit CO Capt Harry C. Crim with a short squadron to perform its share of the escort duties. His Red Flight was first to reach the target area, and he soon spotted about 30 enemy interceptors of various types, all operating independently of each other. Among those Japanese fighters was the Ki-61 flown by Cpl Tomonobu Matsueda of 244th Sentai. Crim made the following report of the ensuing action, which likely involved Matsueda:

My flight was over a bomber box just south of Tokyo when a Zeke was reported at "6 o'clock high." My flight turned 180 degrees, and the Zeke passed overhead. At this time, I saw a Tony going in the opposite direction about 1,000ft lower. I made an overhead attack on him but couldn't get the right amount of lead, so on the recovery from 500ft below I gave him a short burst from close range. Overshooting, I pulled up over him and rolled on my back. From this position I could see the left side of his engine burning. He then started about a one-needle-width turn to the left, and I dropped back on his tail. From this position I fired a three- or four-second burst from about 300ft. His right wing came off at the middle panel.

When VII Fighter Command tallied the results of its first mission, Brig Gen "Mickey" Moore had reason to be pleased, despite the fact that a mechanical problem had forced him to abort the flight. The Mustang pilots were credited with 26 Japanese aircraft destroyed, one probably destroyed and five damaged. The cost was two P-51s and one pilot (1Lt Robert Anderson of the 531st FS) lost. Only three Superfortresses went down (Oyake's ramming victim and two hit by anti-aircraft fire) on April 7.

VII Fighter Command claims were somewhat inflated, as the IJAAF reported 11 fighters destroyed, and the IJNAF's 302nd Kokutai lost five more to the P-51s. But the Japanese claims were even more inaccurate, including 14 destroyed and 40 damaged (P-51s and B-29s) by the IJAAF alone.

APRIL 12, 1945

Five days after their initial mission to Tokyo, VII Fighter Command Mustangs escorted 94 B-29s back to the Nakajima factory for another crack at it. Weather problems dogged the P-51s, forcing one squadron to return to base without reaching Japan and leaving 82 Mustangs to complete the mission.

Despite having trouble rendezvousing with the strung-out formation of B-29s in hazy skies, the P-51 pilots managed to thwart the efforts of the Japanese interceptors. Maj Fred Shirley, CO of the 46th FS/21st FG, made first contact and shot down a Ki-45 that was attempting to close on the Superfortresses. Shirley, a combat veteran who had completed 19 missions in P-40s during the Marshall Islands campaign, reformed his flight and went after a V-formation of J2Ms. In the short fight that followed, Shirley claimed his second victory of the day, and two others went to 1Lts John Brock and Eugene Nabor, while Capt Jack Garnett claimed a probable.

Capt Jim Tapp, operations officer of the 78th FS/15th FG, enjoys a sandwich and a cup of coffee after returning to Iwo Jima following the April 7, 1945 VLR mission, during which he had downed four enemy aircraft over Tokyo. Five days later Tapp scored his fifth confirmed victory to become the first ace of VII Fighter Command. One of the most skilled and respected fighter leaders in the Seventh Air Force, Tapp, who claimed eight victories in total, finished the war as the CO of the 78th FS. (USAF)

Maj Fred Shirley, CO of the 46th FS/21st FG, scored the four aerial victories shown here on his Mustang before the end of April 1945. In addition to flying with VII Fighter Command, Shirley completed 16 missions with the 45th FS/15th FG in P-40Ns during the Marshall Islands campaign in early 1944. (Author's Collection)

The 21st FG's 72nd FS failed to contact any enemy aircraft over the target, but on reaching the rally point for their return flight to Iwo Jima, a particularly daring J2M pilot attacked the Mustangs and shot down 1Lt James Beattie, who was killed.

The 15th FG claimed 11 victories in the dogfights of April 12. The most significant of these was scored by Capt Jim Tapp of the 78th FS. He was leading his flight at the extreme right flank of the formation when he spotted a Ki-61 Hein below him and shot it down in a diving pass. This was Tapp's fifth confirmed victory in two missions, making him the first ace of VII Fighter Command. Sadly, Tapp's wingman, 1Lt Fred White, was following him so closely that spent shells from Tapp's guns were apparently sucked into the air scoop under White's Mustang and damaged its radiator. White's engine failed on his flight home and he bailed out, only for his parachute to fail. White fell to his death. Fellow 78th FS pilot 1Lt Gordon Christoe was also lost.

The mission of April 12 was unusual in that VII Fighter Command's tally of 15 kills was actually fewer than the 17 losses that the IJAAF and IJNAF suffered that day, according to Japanese sources. 302nd Kokutai reported six Raidens damaged against one B-29 probably destroyed and another damaged. No B-29s were lost.

APRIL 19, 1945

VII Fighter Command had another surprise in store for its opponents when 106 Mustangs from the 15th and 21st FGs arrived over Japan on April 19 in the first of what would become a familiar mission profile. This time, the Japanese interceptor pilots found no B-29s to attack, just a swarm of P-51s on a sweep of the IJNAF's Atsugi and Yokosuka airfields. Another weakness of the Japanese air defense system had allowed this surprise, because the radar sites on Honshu were unable to differentiate between large aircraft such as B-29s and smaller fighters. Now, although the defenders had been ordered to avoid combat with the P-51s, they would have to fight it out.

While the 15th FG maintained altitude as top cover, the 21st FG Mustangs swept down toward Atsugi, its three squadrons each spreading out in line abreast formation as they sped toward the target at 400mph. They found 150–200 aircraft of all types parked on the airfield, and proceeded to tear into them, claiming 14 destroyed and 53 damaged. As they pulled off the target, the 46th and 72nd FSs jumped a formation of Nakajima J1N1 Gekko (Moonlight) "Irving" twin-engined naval fighters and claimed nine destroyed. The 531st FS Mustangs found some training aircraft flying nearby and shot down several of them before heading for home.

Although caught by surprise, the IJNAF was able to scramble 19 J2Ms and ten A6Ms from 302nd Kokutai to oppose the raiding Mustangs. By this time, the 15th FG had dropped from its top cover perch to attack the Raidens. Lt(jg) Sadaaki Akamatsu was leading a flight of four J2Ms over the Sagami River when they encountered 20 P-51s and attempted to attack. His wingman was lining up on a Mustang when Akamatsu warned him of a second USAAF fighter closing from behind. The Raidens broke off and escaped, but others were not so fortunate.

Against the Mustang pilots' claims of five destroyed and two damaged, 302nd Kokutai reported three J2Ms shot down and another severely damaged. One of the IJNAF pilots lost was Lt(jg) Akira Fukuda. Among the US pilots claiming a Raiden kill that day was Capt F. H. "Herb" Henderson of the 45th FS, who reported:

Lt(jg) Sadaaki Akamatsu first clashed with Mustangs of VII Fighter Command on April 19, 1945, when he led a flight of four J2M3s in an attack on 20 USAAF fighters over the Sagami River. That day, 106 P-51Ds had been sortied to target the IJNAF's airfields at Atsugi and Yokosuka. The 35-year-old Akamatsu claimed two Mustangs destroyed following the brief engagement with the American aircraft. (Tony Holmes Collection)

I was the leader of a flight that also consisted of John Kester, Don Statsmann and a fourth pilot who may have aborted on takeoff. We were ready to return to Iwo Jima when I spotted two J2M "Jacks" headed toward the mainland. We gave chase, and the three of us took shots at the trailing "Jack." I made a pass at him, scoring hits, but had to break off because I overran him. Kester was next to score hits, but he too overran and had to break off. Statsmann finally finished him off. The "Jack" literally started coming apart and spun into the water. We split the credit three ways.

I still had the lead "Jack" in sight and went after him. When I got in range I began spraying him. He headed for the deck, making violent turns right and left. I managed to catch him in a steep turn to the right and got fatal hits on him. My gun camera confirmed the kill. We were over land by that time.

As I broke off, I found that I was alone. I had lost both my wingman and my element leader in the chase. As a matter of fact, I did not see another Mustang anywhere. The en route weather to Iwo became so bad I was flying on instruments. I broke into a clear space and spotted a B-29. I closed on him and asked if he would drop me off at Iwo. I flew on his wing through weather until he let down and pointed to the left, and there was Iwo. What a great group the B-29 guys were.

MAY 29, 1945

In the three-plus months of combat over Japan that followed the April 19 operation, VII Fighter Command would perform only nine more escort missions – the remaining 34 (79 percent) would be fighter sweeps. On May 29, the USAAF made its first attack on Japan's great port on Tokyo Bay, Yokohama. This time, a massive force of 454 B-29s would firebomb the city's industrial area, with 101 Mustangs of the 15th and 21st FGs providing escort. IJAAF and IJNAF interceptors responded in force, setting the scene for what would turn out to be one of the biggest aerial battles of the Pacific War – and the most fruitful day for aerial victories that VII Fighter Command ever recorded.

The Mustangs took off from Iwo Jima at 0630 hrs for the long trip north, dropping to 2,000ft at one point to pass under a nasty weather front, before climbing to their escort altitude of 20,000ft to rendezvous with the B-29s. The bombers arrived at 1000 hrs and the Mustangs spread out over them as the huge formation headed east from Mount Fuji on a vector toward the target. The Japanese defenders had received sufficient warning of the incoming raid, and soon the sky was dotted with bursting anti-aircraft fire and small formations of intercepting fighters. Within minutes, Mustangs and Japanese fighters were tangling at points all around the B-29s.

Although most of the fighting involved single-engined aircraft of both sides, a formation of 53rd Sentai Ki-45s managed to intercept the B-29s, with devastating results. The unit claimed 11 B-29s shot down for the loss of one Ki-45, likely the victim of 1Lt Charles Cameron of the 47th FS/15th FG.

Capt Robert W. "Todd" Moore was leading a 45th FS flight covering the lead section of Superfortresses, having just transferred back to the unit from the 78th FS. He spotted three J2M Raidens at "ten o'clock high" and went after them, instructing his second element to attack the No. 3 Raiden while he chased the leader. Moore fired a deflection shot and saw immediate hits, followed by the pilot bailing out. The No. 2 Raiden peeled off into a steep dive, and Moore followed. His Mustang overtook the J2M, and he fired a telling burst from a range of about 300 yards that sent it crashing into the ground. Moore's element leader, Capt Jay Slater, claimed the third Raiden as probably destroyed.

It is possible these were the three J2Ms lost by 302nd Kokutai that day, including one flown by Lt(jg) Seijo Boji, who was killed. 302nd claimed no victories. Other Japanese pilots known to have perished were CPOs Nobuyuki Tanabe and Jun-ichi Hoshino of 601st Kokutai and CPO Takao Kate of 252nd Kokutai.

Reforming his flight, Moore patrolled along the bomber stream for several minutes before spotting two N1K2-J Shiden-Kai circling over Yokohama. As Moore approached, one of the fighters dove away while the other attempted to circle in behind the Mustang. Moore broke into a tight turn and eventually closed in behind the Shiden-Kai, firing a short burst into its wing. A second burst hit the fighter squarely, as a result of which its pilot bailed out. While this was going on, Lt(jg) Sadaaki Akamatsu, flying an A6M Zero-sen, made a daring attack on the Mustang flight and shot down Moore's wingman, 2Lt Rufus Moore, before making good his escape.

P-51D-20 MUSTANG COCKPIT

1. Landing gear control lever
2. Elevator trim tab control wheel
3. Carburetor hot air control lever
4. Carburetor cold air control lever
5. Rudder trim tab control
6. Aileron trim tab control
7. Coolant radiator control switch
8. Oil radiator control switch
9. Landing light switch
10. Fluorescent light switch, left
11. Flare pistol port cover
12. Arm rest
13. Mixture control lever
14. Throttle quadrant locks
15. Throttle control
16. Propeller pitch control
17. Selector dimmer assembly
18. Instrument lights
19. Rear radar warning lamp
20. K-14A gunsight
21. Laminated glass
22. Remote compass indicator
23. Clock

24. Suction gauge
25. Manifold pressure gauge
26. Airspeed indicator
27. Directional gyro turn indicator
28. Artificial horizon
29. Coolant temperature
30. Tachometer
31. Altimeter
32. Turn-and-bank indicator
33. Rate-of-climb indicator
34. Carburetor temperature
35. Engine temperature gauge
36. Bomb release levers
37. Engine control panel
38. Landing gear indicator lights
39. Parking brake handle
40. Oxygen flow indicator
41. Oxygen pressure gauge
42. Ignition switch
43. Bomb and rocket switches
44. Cockpit light control
45. Rocket control panel
46. Fuel shut-off valve

47. Fuel selector valve
48. Emergency hydraulic release handle
49. Hydraulic pressure gauge
50. Oxygen hose
51. Oxygen regulator
52. Canopy release handle
53. Canopy crank
54. IFF control panel
55. IFF detonator buttons
56. VHF radio control box
57. Rear radar control panel
58. VHF volume control
59. Fluorescent light switch, right
60. Electrical control panel
61. Circuit breakers
62. BC-438 beacon receiver control box
63. Cockpit light
64. Circuit breakers
65. Rudder pedals
66. Control column
67. Flaps control lever
68. Pilot's seat
69. Flare gun storage

On May 29, 1945, 101 P-51Ds took off from Iwo Jima to escort 454 B-29s tasked with undertaking a high-altitude firebombing raid on Yokohama. The Mustangs met the bombers about 100 miles south of the target at 20,000ft and proceeded towards Yokohama. Defending IJAAF and IJNAF fighters were airborne and ready to strike when the USAAF aircraft reached their Initial Point for the attack. The Japanese pilots initially made head-on passes at the B-29s, but then their USAAF counterparts drew them into a large dogfight that spread across the sky. On the far side of the bomber stream, the 72nd FS/21st FG held its position throughout the B-29s' bomb run. Capt Jim Van Nada, leading four Mustangs in P-51D-20 44-63756 *SHARPIE*, later reported:

"We observed two formations of single-engined planes about 10,000ft below. We nosed over to identify [them], and shortly could see the radial engines and Japanese markings. We picked up considerable speed from our altitude advantage. I started firing from about 1,000ft range and observed hits on the trailing Tojo. He started breaking up, with large pieces of cowling and canopy flying off. I continued firing to within about 100ft and made a steep pullout to avoid hitting him or the debris. The rest of the Tojos made a tight turn to the left as my wingman, Lt Louis Pendergrass, was firing at the last one. I called for him to reform because two Tojos of the lead formation were starting a pass at us from our seven o'clock position. We still had speed advantage and left them in trail while heading for the rendezvous."

With more than 600 aircraft involved, the clash over Yokohama on May 29, 1945 may have been the biggest single aerial battle of the Pacific War.

Capt Moore's three confirmed victories were two better than the one claimed by ace Maj Jim Tapp of the 78th FS, giving him the scoring lead among VII Fighter Command pilots with nine kills. He never relinquished this, finishing the war with 12 victories. Overall, the Mustang pilots claimed 28 confirmed victories for the loss of three P-51s and one pilot, making the mission of May 29, 1945, the most successful VII Fighter Command operation of them all.

Luck turned against the Mustang pilots on the following Friday, June 1, when 24 of them went down in a huge storm while attempting to reach Japan on VLR Mission Number 15.

JUNE 10, 1945

A new fighter group shared escort duties with the 21st FG on this date when 280 B-29s attacked aircraft factories in the Tokyo area. The 506th FG, which had formed in Florida in October 1944 with the specific purpose of training for VLR operations, arrived on Iwo Jima in mid-May, flew its first mission on the 28th and lost 11 pilots in the weather debacle on June 1. A better day lay ahead.

Nearly 120 Japanese fighters rose to challenge the incoming American raid. Among the defenders were the IJNAF's 302nd Kokutai (J2Ms and A6Ms), 601st Kokutai (A6Ms) and Sento 402nd Hikotai (A6Ms), as well as the IJAAF's 52nd Sentai (Ki-84s) and 244th Sentai (Ki-61s and Ki-100s). Other units may have also been involved. As the Japanese fighters climbed in uncoordinated fashion, the Mustangs pounced from their escort altitude of 23,000ft. The result was a lopsided victory for VII Fighter Command, with scores of 24 aircraft confirmed destroyed, four probables, and seven damaged for no losses. More importantly, no B-29s were lost either.

One of the American pilots scoring his first victory that day was Maj Tom DeJarnette, mission leader of the 506th FG and CO of the 462nd FS. He spotted a formation of Ki-61 Heins attempting to close on the B-29s and led his flight of Mustangs into the attack in defense of the bombers:

I picked out the first one and could see my bullets all over his plane. I broke off when he started smoking. I gathered my flight and started climbing to cover the B-29s when another Tony was sighted headed in the direction of the bombers. We climbed right on him, and [Darrell] Bash, Rosie [Roseborough] and I got good hits. He started smoking, spun, and crashed into a mountain.

1Lt Bash got credit for the second Ki-61.

DeJarnette's victory had been a long time coming. He was one of the few pilots in the 506th FG with combat experience, having flown a full combat tour on P-39s in New Guinea during 1942 without making a single claim. Despite his long-awaited personal success on the mission, DeJarnette was dissatisfied with his pilots' overall "poor air discipline." In debriefing, he told his pilots they had flown too close together, had been too individualistic and not watchful enough, and that the wingmen had not paid close enough attention to their leaders' flying. Nevertheless, 506th FG pilots were credited with 11 confirmed victories.

Japanese pilots known to have been killed in action on June 10 included CPO Naraichi Murai (601st Kokutai), WO Takio Yoshida (Sento 402nd Hikotai), Capt Shio Ban-Nai (52nd Sentai), and Sgt Setsuho Takada (244th Sentai).

JUNE 23, 1945

Weather continued to wreak havoc with flight operations from Iwo Jima as the monsoon season took hold, so it was nearly two weeks before VII Fighter Command was given the opportunity for its next crack at the Japanese. This time it was a strike by 99 Mustangs of the 15th and 506th FGs against Shimodate, Kasumigahara, Hyakurigahara, and Katori airfields in the Tokyo area.

For once, the Japanese defenders held the advantage when the American fighters approached their targets, perhaps because the local radar operators had mistaken the Mustangs for Superfortresses when they raised the alarm. As on June 10, around 120 Japanese fighters scrambled, and with sufficient time to climb, many of them were above the P-51s when they attacked. Despite their initial advantage, the Japanese defenders were unable to capitalize on the situation.

Ki-84s, likely from 51st or 52nd Sentai, struck first when they bounced the 47th FS near the coast. Flying top cover for the other two 15th FG squadrons,

A pair of Mustangs from the 458th FS/506th FG close up with an F-13 Superfortress conducting a photo-reconnaissance mission over the Home Islands in June 1945. The 506th was the final Mustang-equipped group to see action from Iwo Jima, flying its first mission on May 28, 1945. Four days later, the unit lost 11 pilots in the weather debacle of June 1. (NARA)

Capt Fumisuke Shono taxies out in a Ki-61-Ib at a snowy Chiran. Note the camouflaged ailerons and remnants of camouflage on the white Homeland Defense "bandages" on the wings. 244th Sentai aircraft went through stages of being camouflaged, stripped of paint and re-camouflaged. Shono was shot down by a Mustang while flying a Ki-100 in defense of airfields in the Nagoya area on July 16, 1945. He had claimed a pair of P-51s immediately prior to bailing out of his mortally damaged fighter. (Tony Holmes Collection)

the 47th fought back as the 45th and 78th FSs let down to begin their runs over their assigned target airfields. In the ensuing dogfight, the 47th FS scored 11 confirmed victories for the loss of three P-51s and one pilot. Top scorer was 1Lt Bob Scamara with three victories, one probable, and six damaged.

The 506th FG trailed the 15th over Japan, and it got a similar reception as the top cover 458th FS fought off diving Japanese interceptors while the 457th and 462nd FSs proceeded with rocket attacks on two airfields. The 458th FS pilots were credited with ten victories for no losses. 1Lt Bill Ebersole of the 462nd FS gave a detailed description of his squadron's technique for airfield strafing attacks:

I still get goose bumps thinking back on the excitement of diving down from 20,000ft at close to full throttle, leveling out at tree-top height as one of a dozen airplanes lined up abreast, and racing across an airfield with guns blazing. We each had six 0.50-cal machine guns. Every fifth round of ammunition was a tracer bullet, with two incendiary and two armor-piercing bullets making up the other four of each five rounds. With the tracer ricocheting in all directions, the incendiary rounds exploding when they hit, explosions on the ground and a mass of return fire from enemy flak gunners, it would put any 4th of July finale to shame.

JULY 9, 1945

By late June 1945 it was becoming obvious to VII Fighter Command that the frequency and intensity of Japanese intercepts of American raids on Honshu were diminishing. This was due in part to losses suffered by the defenders in three months of combat with USAAF Mustangs, plus dwindling supplies of fuel. Another factor was the Imperial Supreme War Command's implementation of Operation *Ketsu Go* for maximum defense with a minimum number of interceptors. This would allow the IJAAF and IJNAF to pull most of their forces out of range of the American raiders to save them for use during the Allies' expected invasion of the Home Islands.

This did not dissuade VII Fighter Command from continuing to pound Japanese targets on Honshu, however. A fighter strike on July 9 to Osaka produced 13 confirmed aerial victories for the 21st FG, including two by Capt Willis Mathews, for no losses. As the group's three squadrons ran in on the target, they unwittingly sandwiched two large formations of Japanese fighters between the 531st FS, flying top cover, and the 46th and 72nd FSs below. The 531st dove on the enemy aircraft, which split-essed into a thin layer of cloud and emerged among the two strike squadrons underneath. A wild, one-sided melee ensued, with the Japanese getting the worst of it.

The IJAAF's 56th Sentai, in its only encounter with P-51s and its last combat of the war, lost three Ki-61s and two pilots, Lt Kazuo Nozaki and Sgt Maj Tomotoshi Fuji. WO Tadao Sumi claimed one Mustang destroyed, although none were lost.

WO Tadao Sumi, a Ki-61 pilot with 56th Sentai, claimed one Mustang destroyed on July 9, 1945, although none were lost that day. He also claimed four B-29s destroyed and three damaged in the course of several missions on the night of March 13–14, 1945. As a direct result of these successes, Sumi was awarded an individual citation and the prestigious Bukosho, First Class. The latter can be seen here pinned to the left breast pocket of his flying overall. An IJAAF decoration, the Bukosho was established on December 7, 1944 by Imperial edict. Just 89 had been awarded by war's end. (Tony Holmes Collection)

JULY 16, 1945

If the Japanese were scaling back their air defense effort, it was not obvious on July 16, 1945, when Mustangs of the 21st and 506th FGs crossed the coastline to attack airfields in the Nagoya area. Led by Lt Col John Mitchell of VII Fighter Command, the 21st FG reached the target area first and encountered an estimated 60 Japanese fighters before the Mustangs were able to strafe. The 506th FG, led by group operations officer Maj Malcolm "Muddy" Watters, joined the battle a few moments later.

VII Fighter Command publication *Fighter Notes* later described the Japanese defenders as more "aggressive and able" during this encounter than on any previous mission. "However, they did not use mutual support, and our airplanes always had the advantage except when they became separated, and several Japs could attack a stray Mustang."

The 506th FG reported four Mustangs damaged in the fight, but more importantly, 457th FS operations officer Capt John Benbow was killed. His victor was almost certainly Maj Yohei Hinoki of the Akeno Kyodo Hikoshidan Training Air Division), whose 2nd Daitai had scrambled with 24 Ki-100s mostly flown by inexperienced trainees. Upon reaching 23,000ft over Ise Bay, Hinoki spotted the Mustang formations below. A veteran ace who had seen action from December 7, 1941, he had lost his lower right leg in an aerial battle with P-51As over Burma in November 1943 and had subsequently learned to fly with an artificial limb, although he had been confined to instructor duties since then. Hinoki gave the following detailed account of the action on July 16:

Maj Yohei Hinoki, a former 64th Sentai ace who had lost his lower right leg fighting P-51As over Burma in November 1943, later served as an instructor with 2nd Daitai of Akeno Kyodo Hikoshidan. His final tally of 11 victories included a B-29 and a P-51D, the latter being downed on July 16, 1945, while Hinoki was at the controls of a Ki-100. (Tony Holmes Collection)

At around 1000 hrs, we received information about enemy movement – there was a group of small aircraft flying toward Ise Bay, near Nagoya. My group had 12 aircraft, consisting of Sugiyama flight [four aircraft], Mihara flight [four aircraft], and my flight [four aircraft]. Eto group [led by fellow ace Maj Toyoki Eto] also had 12 aircraft, and we took off together that morning to fight the approaching P-51s.

Flying high, I kept my aircraft above and to the right of the Eto group. We flew over Shinmiya and then turned left, flying along the coastline heading for Shima-Hanto. At an altitude of about 7,000m, just above Ise Shrine, Sugiyama flight turned to the right toward the ocean, and the distance between our flights and Eto's group grew. Then we sighted the P-51 group flying well below us just above the ocean. They looked so small, just like floating strings.

All of a sudden, Sugiyama flight headed downward straight into the P-51s. I sped up in order to stay with them, and to provide cover for their attack. I saw the P-51 group make a sudden turn. There were 11 aircraft in three flights. I approached the last plane with the thought of revenge for my leg, which I had lost in Burma. I noticed that my aircraft was sliding around a lot because of a propeller problem that arose when I opened the throttle.

Despite pressing my artificial leg hard down against the rudder pedal, I still felt frustration at not having any real control over this limb. I dived down on the enemy plane, approaching until I could see the pilot's white teeth. Even if my plane skidded, I couldn't miss. At a distance of no more than 20m, I fired several times. The plane soon dove away out of control, spinning down as if in its death struggle. It was easy for us to shoot these P-51s down, for their sole defensive maneuver was to perform a circular turn. The Ki-100 had a superior turning circle in comparison with the P-51, and we simply cut inside their defensive turns.

The enemy planes had come to attack the Kyuko area, but they were forced to alter their mission due to our interception. Our 24 aircraft had intercepted around 250 American planes, and we would have easily won this fight if we had had more experienced pilots within our group. In order to prevail, we had to fight as a group, but instead we fought individually and lost three great pilots.

I soon found myself surrounded by 15 enemy aircraft, all of which were shooting at me. I made a series of sharp circular turns in an effort to avoid being hit. When I decided to withdraw, the leader of the enemy aircraft that surrounded me commenced a series of aggressive maneuvers in an effort to finish me off. I responded with yet another sequence of tight circular turns, but soon realized that I couldn't escape. In desperation, I pushed my plane over into a vertical dive and opened the throttle. Despite my body being subjected to an incredible build-up of air pressure, the aircraft remained fully controllable, and when I pulled out of the dive I was totally alone. The fight had lasted a full 50 minutes.

We destroyed 11 enemy aircraft [only Benbow was in fact shot down], but lost three pilots in return [the Mustang pilots claimed five victories]. Considering that our small team was only newly assembled and fighting against such a large group of enemy aircraft, the loss of three pilots was not so bad. We owed this result principally to our aircraft, which we called the Goshikisen.

As noted, the 457th FS pilots claimed five victories (exactly the number lost by 2nd Daitai), which they identified as "Ki-84s" and a "Ki-44." Given the unfamiliarity of the Ki-100 to the American pilots (it was so new that the Allies never assigned it a reporting name), it is likely that several of the losses were Hinoki's students. Another Ki-100 pilot shot down was Capt Fumisuke Shono of 244th Sentai. Although he claimed two victories before being forced to take to his parachute, Capt Benbow's Mustang was the only loss of the day.

Every squadron in the two American fighter groups claimed victories during the July 16 mission, with the final score being 22 confirmed kills, two probables, and 17 damaged. This proved to be VII Fighter Command's last double-digit victory total of the war, and two squadrons – the 46th and 531st FSs – actually recorded their last claims that day.

A Ki-100-Ib of Akeno Kyodo Hikoshidan. This aircraft was flown by instructor 1Lt Mamoru Tatsuda, and it is similar in appearance to the Goshikisen used by Maj Yohei Hinoki to down a Mustang on July 16, 1945. The instructors serving with Akeno Kyodo Hikoshidan were called on to occasionally fly combat missions before the unit was reformed as 111th Sentai in late July 1945. (John W. Lambert Collection/Museum of Flight)

1. Army Type 100 reflector gunsight
2. Airspeed indicator
3. Turn-and-bank indicator
4. Rate-of-climb indicator
5. Manifold pressure gauge
6. Compass
7. Altimeter
8. Tachometer
9. Fuel pressure gauge
10. Oil pressure gauge
11. Oil temperature gauge
12. Landing gear indicator lights
13. Type 1 (Ho-103) 12.7mm machine guns
14. Cabin lamps

15. Elevator trim control
16. Hydraulic pressure gauge
17. Radio tuner
18. Cylinder temperature gauge
19. Exhaust temperature gauge
20. Control column
21. Canopy winding mechanism
22. "Butterfly" flaps control buttons
23. Main switches
24. Oxygen control
25. Oxygen flow meter
26. Fuel gauge (main tanks)
27. Fuel gauge (auxiliary tanks)
28. Left and right auxiliary tank selector

29. Left and right main tank selector
30. Pilot's seat
31. Hydrostatic plunger for main tanks
32. Hydrostatic plungers for auxiliary tanks
33. Hydraulic brake pedals
34. Rudder pedals
35. P.4 compass
36. Emergency hydraulic hand pump
37. Magneto switch
38. Throttle lever
39. Mixture control
40. Propeller pitch control

41. Friction adjuster
42. Internal tanks cock
43. Main fuel cock
44. Undercarriage emergency operation handle
45. Cam manipulation handle
46. Undercarriage selector switch
47. Flap selector handle
48. Compressed air bottle
49. Clock
50. Flap position indicator
51. Hydraulic brake pressure gauge

One of the IJNAF pilots who was credited with a P-51 kill was Lt Yutaka Morioka of 302nd Kokutai. After his left hand was lost in combat fighting B-29s in January 1945 (his arm is bandaged up in this photograph), Morioka had it replaced by a hook. He claimed his fifth, and last, victory on August 3, 1945, when he downed the P-51D flown by 2Lt John J. Coneff whilst flying an A6M7. (John W. Lambert Collection/ Museum of Flight)

AUGUST 3, 1945

With what remained of the Japanese interceptor force going into hiding, VII Fighter Command Mustangs were free to roam at will over Honshu in search of lucrative targets. The low-level work had its own risks, however, as Japanese anti-aircraft gunners, particularly those defending airfields, became increasingly skilled and deadly.

On August 3, 1945, 97 Mustangs spread out across the Kanto Plain at treetop level to attack airfields around Tokyo. The anti-aircraft defenses were ready for them, and by the time the raid ended, the USAAF had lost four P-51Ds, with a further 13 damaged.

One of the ground fire victims, 1Lt Ed Mikes of the 458th FS/506th FG, managed to bail out over Sagami-Wan, where a B-17 "Super Dumbo" rescue aircraft dropped a motorboat to him while two US Navy PB4Y Privateers and a submarine-cover flight from the 457th FS/506th FG orbited overhead at 3,500ft. All this activity drew the attention of Japanese ground spotters across the bay at Yokosuka, and a flight of four 302nd Kokutai A6M7s was scrambled from Atsugi in response. Leading the fighters was Lt Yutaka Morioka, who had recently returned to flight status after losing his left hand (replaced by a hook) in combat with a B-29 in January. He described the action that followed in a letter to historian Henry Sakaida many years later:

Capt Abner Aust, a flight commander of the 457th FS/506th FG, scored five confirmed victories to become the group's only ace. His last two successes came on August 10, 1945, when he was credited with two A6Ms destroyed. Aust flew some 300 combat missions over Vietnam later in his career. (Author's Collection)

I and three other pilots flew to Atami, and I found there in the bright sunshine a rubber boat and an approaching submarine. Above them were two B-24s [PB4Ys] and higher still four P-51s guarding. We approached the P-51s from the rear and higher; the P-51s did not spot us, nor did the submarine open fire. From a distance of about 500m, I fired my 13mm guns at the P-51 at the extreme left of the formation to find the range, then at about 100m I fired my 20mm guns, hitting the P-51. Fearing a collision, I zoomed up. Looking down, I saw three P-51s and a big, white circle on the surface of the water.

A 70th Sentai 3rd Chutai Ki-44-IIb in flight over the Kanto Plain. This aircraft appears to have had its wing armament removed. 70th Sentai, based at Kashiwa, was a mainstay of IJAAF fighter defenses over Japan from May 1943. That month it re-equipped with the Shoki, and the Nakajima fighter was retained though to war's end. By then, 70th Sentai had claimed 120 American aircraft destroyed or damaged for the loss of 17 pilots. (Tony Holmes Collection)

Morioka's victim was 2Lt John J. Coneff, who was killed. Morioka and his flight continued chasing the P-51s without success and then strafed Capt Mikes in his lifeboat during their return flight to Atsugi. Shortly afterwards, the submarine USS *Aspro* picked up Mikes and made its escape from Sagami-Wan.

AUGUST 10, 1945

Despite the devastation wrought by the atomic attacks on Hiroshima (August 6) and Nagasaki (August 9), the Japanese government hesitated to accept the peace terms demanded by the Allies, and the aerial assault on the Home Islands continued. On August 10, P-51Ds of VII Fighter Command escorted 70 B-29s to Tokyo for the first time in six weeks.

Just before the bombers arrived over their target (a Tokyo arsenal complex), a mixed force of IJAAF and IJNAF fighters made an uncoordinated and disorganized attack that was easily countered by the Mustangs of the 15th and 506th FGs. Among the seven confirmed victories credited to pilots was one to Maj Todd Moore, now 45th FS commander, bringing his total to 12 and making him the top ace of VII Fighter Command. The other notable success that day was by Capt Abner Aust of the 457th FS, who claimed two A6Ms for his fourth and fifth victories, making him the only ace of the 506th FG and the last ace of VII Fighter Command. Capt Kanji Honda, executive officer of Ki-44-equipped 70th Sentai, was one of the pilots killed in action on August 10.

Four days later, the Mustangs returned to Tokyo on another escort, and this time the skies were vacant of Japanese interceptors. The anti-aircraft batteries were active, however, and 2Lt Phil Schlamberg of the 78th FS/15th FG was shot down and killed over Futugawa. Less than an hour later, during the flight home, mission leader Maj Todd Moore heard the code word "UTAH" broadcast over his radio. The war was over.

STATISTICS AND ANALYSIS

When pilots of VII Fighter Command flew their first mission over Japan on April 7, 1945, neither they nor their Japanese counterparts that they encountered could guess the campaign that opened that day would last just 13 weeks. Lacking knowledge of the atomic weapons that soon would level Hiroshima and Nagasaki, all assumed the

USAAF records show 214 P-51Ds of VII Fighter Command were lost to all causes during the VLR campaign. 44-63453 *Miss Jo III* of the 78th FS/15th FG looks to be repairable, however, after wiping off its undercarriage following an excursion beyond the tarmac of Airfield No 1's runway in June 1945. (NARA)

war would drag on through a bloody invasion of Japan that would not even begin until fall 1945. Instead, the fighting would come to an abrupt end in mid-August. As a result, the Mustang pilots on Iwo Jima flew just 51 missions (4,172 sorties) over Japan during their VLR campaign of 1945, encountering enemy aircraft on 33 occasions.

It is impossible to reduce the results of the VLR campaign to a comparison of numbers of successes and losses due to the paucity of statistics available from the Japanese side. Not only were most Japanese records destroyed at the end of the war, but also the Japanese and Americans differed in their systems for assessing their respective combat effectiveness. Thus, while we have documentation for VII Fighter Command claims of 227 confirmed victories, 35 probable victories and a further 100 aircraft damaged in aerial combat, plus 700 aircraft destroyed on the ground, no such numbers are available for the Japanese forces involved in the campaign. Nor can we properly assess the accuracy of American claims without Japanese records of their losses.

Major Robert W. "Todd" Moore was the leading ace of VII Fighter Command, scoring 11 victories over Japan in P-51Ds and a previous P-40N kill during the Marshall Islands campaign. Moore commanded the 45th FS/ 15th FG after starting the VLR campaign in the 78th FS. (NARA)

USAAF records show 214 P-51Ds lost to all causes (including air-to-air combat, ground fire, accidents, weather and mechanical failures). Fewer than half of these resulted in losses of American pilots – 86 pilots were killed, including five of the 14 who became prisoners of war. Among those killed were the 24 pilots who went down in the deadly typhoon of June 1 before reaching Japan. The American pilot loss rate of 2.3 percent was substantial but not unsustainable.

One popular misconception about the VLR campaign is that the purpose of the P-51 missions was to provide escort for B-29s attacking Japanese cities. While this may have been the original reason for sending Mustangs to Iwo Jima, P-51s performed only 12 escort missions during VLR operations because by April 1945 most B-29 firebombing strikes were taking place at night. Clashes between Japanese and American fighters dropped off from July, when the Imperial Supreme War Command ordered its fighter forces to avoid combat with P-51s whenever they did not hold a clear tactical advantage.

VII Fighter Command Aces		
Maj Robert W. "Todd" Moore	15th FG	12-1-1 (including 1 victory in 1944)
Lt Col John W. Mitchell	15th and 21st FGs	11-0-0 (including 8 victories with Thirteenth Air Force)
Maj James B. Tapp	15th FG	8-0-2
Maj Harry L. Crim	21st FG	6-0-4
Capt Willis B. Mathews	21st FG	5.5-3.33-3.83 (including 3.5 victories with Twelfth Air Force)
Capt Abner M. Aust	506th FG	5-0-3

IJAAF Pilots claiming P-51 victories

2Lt Makoto Ogawa	70th Sentai	2 victories
Capt Fumiske Shono	244th Sentai	2 victories
Maj Yohei Hinoki	Akeno 2nd Daitai	1 victory
Sgt Shuichi Kaiho	39th Kyoiku Hikotai	1 victory
WO Tadao Sumi	56th Sentai	1 victory

IJNAF pilots claiming P-51 victories

Lt(jg) Sadaaki Akamatsu	302nd Kokutai	3.5 victories
Lt Yutaka Morioka	302nd Kokutai	1 victory
WO Kaneyoshi Muto	Yokosuka Kokutai	1 victory
CPO Toru Saijo	302nd Kokutai	0 5 victory

Another Bukosho recipient, WO Makoto Ogawa of 70th Sentai claimed seven Superfortresses destroyed prior to adding two P-51 Mustangs to his tally. (Tony Holmes Collection)

AFTERMATH

Having suffered serious losses to USAAF and US Navy fighters in the spring of 1945, the Japanese pulled most of their defending aircraft out of combat to save them for kamikaze duty during the impending invasion of the Home Islands by the Allies – an invasion that fortunately never happened. As a result, a sizable number of Japanese aircraft of all types survived the war. Most captured in Japan were destroyed within a few months.

Examples of advanced Japanese frontline fighter types and others still under development were shipped to the US and Britain for evaluation after V-J Day. An example is the Ki-100-Ib now on display in the RAF Museum Midlands at Cosford, in Shropshire. It was flown from Japan to French Indochina in the closing days of the war and captured by the British at Tan Son Nhut (Saigon) airfield. After several test flights, the Ki-100-Ib was one of four Japanese aircraft shipped to Britain in the summer of 1946. Placed in storage and moved several times before being repainted and placed on display at Biggin Hill, in Kent, the fighter was eventually moved to Cosford. It is the only surviving Ki-100 in the world.

Similarly, the only surviving Ki-84 is displayed at Chiran Peace Museum for Kamikaze Pilots in Chiran (Minamikyushu), Japan. American forces captured it at Clark Field, in the Philippines, in 1945. Other Hayate captured in China were flown by the People's Liberation Army Air Force into the 1950s.

Among IJNAF fighters, the sole surviving Raiden served with 302nd Kokutai at Atsugi. Following the Japanese surrender in September 1945, this J2M3 was sent to the US for performance tests. It was later acquired by a trade school in Los Angeles as an instructional airframe and currently resides at the Planes of Fame Air Museum in Chino, California. Four N1K2-J Shiden-Kai survive, including one at the National Museum of the US Air Force in Dayton, Ohio, and another at the National Naval Aviation Museum in Pensacola, Florida.

With the end of the war, most Japanese aircraft in the Home Islands were destroyed by the victorious Allied forces. This Ki-100-Ib, the only one in existence, was spared by the British and now resides in the RAF Museum Midlands at Cosford, in Shropshire. (Tony Holmes Collection)

After the surrender, the IJAAF and IJNAF were disbanded and US and Allied armed forces took control of Japanese military bases. Yokota Air Base, located west of Tokyo and formerly called Tama airfield, eventually became a major USAF base and was used for combat missions over North and South Korea during the Korean War. Iwo Jima, on the other hand, was returned to Japan with the Bonin Islands in 1968. The island has no permanent inhabitants except those at a Self-Defense Force base on its Central Field.

Although NAA continued to develop Mustang variants after the war, the D-model (renamed F-51D in 1948) served long after the others were retired. Mustang fighter-bombers took a heavy toll on communist forces during the first 18 months of the Korean War. Many foreign air forces flew Mustangs in the post-war era, and a handful remained in operation into the early 1980s with smaller air arms. The last military F-51D was retired by the Dominican Air Force in 1984. Of the roughly 15,000 Mustangs of all models produced, around 150 are still flying worldwide, the aircraft remaining popular attractions at airshows and air races to this day.

FURTHER READING

BOOKS

Hata, Ikuhiko, Izawa, Yasuho and Shores, Christopher, *Japanese Army Air Force Fighter Units and Their Aces 1931–1945* (Grub Street, 2002)

Hata, Ikuhiko, Izawa, Yasuho and Shores, Christopher, *Japanese Naval Air Force Fighter Units and Their Aces 1932–1945* (Grub Street, 2011)

Holmes, Tony, *Osprey Duel 91 – Hellcat vs Shiden/Shiden-Kai Pacific Theater 1944–45* (Osprey Publishing Ltd, 2019)

Izawa, Yasuho with Holmes, Tony, *Osprey Aircraft of the Ace 129 – J2M Raiden and N1K1/2 Shiden/Shiden-Kai Aces* (Osprey Publishing Ltd, 2016)

Kuwahara, Yasuo and Allred, Gordon T., *Kamikaze* (Ballantine Books, 1957)

Lambert, John W., *The Long Campaign – The History of the 15th Fighter Group in World War II* (Sunflower University Press, 1982)

Lambert, John W., *The Pineapple Air Force – Pearl Harbor to Tokyo* (Phalanx Publishing Co. Ltd, 1990)

Millman, Nicholas, *Osprey Aircraft of the Aces 100 – Ki-44 'Tojo' Aces of World War II* (Osprey Publishing Ltd, 2011)

Millman, Nicholas, *Osprey Aircraft of the Aces 114 – Ki-61 and Ki-100 Aces* (Osprey Publishing Ltd, 2015)

Molesworth, Carl, Osprey Aviation Elite Units 21 – *Very Long Range P-51 Mustang Units of the Pacific War* (Osprey Publishing Ltd, 2006)

Nijboer, Donald, *Osprey Duel 82 – B-29 Superfortress vs Ki-44 'Tojo' Pacific Theater 1944–45* (Osprey Publishing Ltd, 2017)

Olynyk, Frank J., *USAAF (Pacific Theater) Credits for the Destruction of Enemy Aircraft in Air-To-Air Combat World War 2*, (Frank J. Olynyk, 1985)

Sakai, Saburo with Martin Caiden and Fred Saito, *Samurai* (E. P. Dutton and Co. Inc., 1957)

Sakaida, Henry, *Osprey Aircraft of the Aces 22 – Imperial Japanese Navy Aces 1937–45* (Osprey Publishing Ltd, 1998)

Sakaida, Henry, *Osprey Aircraft of the Aces 13 – Japanese Army Air Force Aces 1937–45* (Osprey Publishing Ltd, 1997)

Taylor, John W. R., *Combat Aircraft of the World* (George Rainbird Ltd, 1969)

Young, Edward M., *Osprey Duel 73 – F4U Corsair vs Ki-84 'Frank' Pacific Theater 1945* (Osprey Publishing Ltd, 2016)

Young, Edward M., *Osprey Duel 62 – F6F Hellcat vs A6M Zero-Sen Pacific Theater 1943–44* (Osprey Publishing Ltd, 2014)

WEBSITES

Interrogations of Japanese Officials – Vols. I and II, United States Strategic Bombing Survey [Pacific]: https://www.history.navy.mil/research/library/online-reading-room/title-list-alphabetically/i/interrogations-japanese-officials-voli.html#no28

Japanese Monograph No. 157, Homeland Air Defense Operations Record: http://ddsnext.crl.edu/titles/31862?terms=&item_id=451270#?c=0&m=159&s=0&cv=1&r=0&xywh=-1661%2C0%2C6559%2C4626

Japanese Aircraft, Ships and Historical Research: www.j-aircraft.com

Nippon Rikukaigun, Imperial Japanese Army and Navy research: https://rikukaigun.org/

VII Fighter Command Sunsetters: https://www.7thfighter.com

PERIODICALS

"VII Fighter Command Compiles Remarkable Record in Past War," *Fighter Post*, October 13, 1945

"Nipponese Uniquity – the story of Kawanishi's Violet Lightning," *Air Enthusiast* (Vol. 4 No. 4) pp. 178–187

Blake, Steve, "Dogfight Over Honshu," *Fighter Pilots in Aerial Combat* (No. 3) pp. 4–6

Blake, Steve, and Henry Sakaida, "Combat Over Japan, Ki-100 vs. P-51" *Fighter Pilots in Aerial Combat* (No. 9) pp. 16–22

Ivie, Tom, "Star of the Seventh," *Air Classics* (Vol. 20 No. 8) pp. 14–27 and 82

INDEX

Note: page locators in **bold** refer to illustrations, captions and plates.